U0901440

故宫博物院藏

# 中国古代窑址标本　浙江（中）

# THE SPECIMENS OF ANCIENT CHINESE KILNS IN THE COLLECTION OF THE PALACE MUSEUM

ZHEJIANG VOLUME　II

故宫博物院编　冯小琦 / 主编

COMPILED BY THE PALACE MUSEUM
THE CHIEF COMPILER: FENG XIAOQI

故　宫　出　版　社
THE FORBIDDEN CITY PUBLISHING HOUSE

# 象山窑

窑址在浙江省象山县，故宫博物院部分专家学者20世纪70年代、80年代及2009年调查了象山黄避岙、白相头窑址。

文献记载象山窑烧白瓷，属于定窑系瓷窑之一。近几年只发现一处唐代青瓷窑址，遗址面积不大，烧瓷时间不长，遗留标本数量较少。多数为不同型、式的盘、碗，还有少量瓶。瓶小口，线条平直，平底。碗以直口平底较多，胎体厚重，多施半釉，式样与丽水、吴兴、余姚及江苏宜兴窑址出土物相同，应属唐代前期江浙地区比较流行的一种碗式。

黄避岙窑。器物风格具唐代特点。有青釉、青黄釉碗、钵、壶等，窑具少量。有的钵为宽唇口，有的釉施至外口沿下，形与宜兴窑相似。窑具有垫饼、喇叭形垫具和支具。

白相头窑。位于象山县城东南14公里，主要烧造青釉碗、瓶。碗胎色深，釉色有青翠、青绿两种，后者色较重，里心有垫圈痕。瓶小口圆唇，身有棱，有的胎质较粗。

# Xiangshan Kiln

Xiangshan kiln is located in Xiangshan County, Zhejiang Province. Experts from the Palace Museum investigated the kiln at Huangbi'ao and Baixiangtou in the 1970s, 1980s and in 2009 respectively.

According to literatures, Xiangshan kiln fired white glaze porcelains. It belonged to the category of Ding kiln. In recent years, only one celadon kiln site of Tang dynasty has been found. The area of the kiln site is not large and the firing history is not long. There are not so many relics left behind. Those left behind are mostly different types of plates, bowls, as well as a small number of vases. Vases are straight with small mouth and flat bottom. Bowls are usually with straight mouth and thick body and half-glazed, with the same shaping as those unearthed from Lishui, Wuxing and Yuyao kiln in Zhejiang Province and Yixing kiln in Jiangsu Province. It should be a popular type of bowl in Jiangsu and Zhejiang Province in earlier Tang dynasty.

Wares fired at Huangbi'ao have clear characteristics of Tang dynasty. The wares are green or yellowish green glaze bowls, alms bowls, pots, etc. Some alms bowls are with wide lip and some are not completely glazed. The outside glazing just stopped under the lip. Its shaping is similar to that of Yixing kiln. There are only a few kiln furniture found, such as pads, speaker-shaped pads and supporting tools.

Located 14 km southeast of Xiangshan County, kiln at Baixiangtouyao fired mainly green glaze bowls and vases. Bowls are with darker body and marks left by supporting ring inside the center. The glaze is in bright green or bluish green and the later is more darker. Vases are with small, round mouth and curved rim. The bodies are decorated with ribs and some of them are poor in quality.

**象山（黄避岙）窑遗址**

Ruin of Xiangshan kiln at Huangbi'ao

521 唐 青釉壶标本
Tang dynasty
Specimen of green glaze pot

522 唐 青釉钵标本
Tang dynasty
Specimens of green glaze alms bowl

523　唐　青釉钵标本
Tang dynasty
Specimen of green glaze alms bowl

524　唐　青釉钵标本
Tang dynasty
Specimens of green glaze alms bowl

525 **唐 青釉钵标本**

Tang dynasty

Specimens of green glaze alms bowl

526　**唐　窑具标本**
Tang dynasty
Specimens of kiln furniture

527　**唐　窑具标本**
Tang dynasty
Specimens of kiln furniture

**象山窑遗址**
Ruin of Xiangshan kiln

528 唐 青釉瓶标本

Tang dynasty

Specimen of green glaze vase

529　唐　青釉罐标本
Tang dynasty
Specimen of green glaze jar

530　唐　青釉罐标本
Tang dynasty
Specimens of green glaze jar

531 唐 青釉双系罐标本
Tang dynasty
Specimens of green glaze jar with two handles

532 唐 青釉碗标本
Tang dynasty
Specimens of green glaze bowl

## 533 唐　青釉碗标本

Tang dynasty

Specimens of green glaze bowl

534 唐 青釉碗标本
Tang dynasty
Specimen of green glaze bowl

535 唐 青釉碗标本
Tang dynasty
Specimen of green glaze bowl

# 宁海窑

2009 年故宫博物院部分专家学者调查了宁海茶院平和下园山窑址。

窑址位于市区南部，青釉标本堆积不多，主要为碗，少量似盒，散布在匣钵等窑具之间。碗里心有长条形不规则的支痕，有的造型很独特。釉色青绿。窑址中有不少 M 形匣钵，匣钵上粘有圈式垫具，圈有大、小之分，但总体上稍大，有的与青釉碗黏结。

# Ninghai Kiln

Experts from the Palace Museum investigated Ninghai kiln sites at Chayuanping and Xiayuanshan in 2009.

The kiln site is located south of the city. There is not so much accumulation at the site. Mainly bowls, together with a small number of boxes might-be were interspersed among kiln furniture of saggars and such. Inside the center of bowls, there is a long, irregular mark left by supporting tool. The shaping of some of the wares is unique. The glaze is in bluish green. There are a lot of M-shaped saggars with supporting rings adhered. The rings vary in size, but in general they are a bit larger. Some of the rings are adhered to green glaze bowls.

宁海（茶院平）窑遗址瓷片遗存
Pileup of porcelain parts at the ruin of Ninghai kiln at Chayuanping

宁海（茶院平）窑遗址瓷片遗存
Pileup of porcelain parts at the ruin of Ninghai kiln at Chayuanping

536　**宋　青釉瓶标本**

Song dynasty

Specimens of green glaze vase

537 **宋 青釉瓶标本**

Song dynasty

Specimens of green glaze vase

538 **宋 青釉瓶标本**

Song dynasty

Specimens of green glaze vase

539　宋　青釉壶标本
Song dynasty
Specimen of green glaze pot

540　宋　窑具标本
Song dynasty
Specimens of kiln furniture

541　五代　青釉碗标本

Five Dynasties

Specimens of green glaze bowl

542 五代 青釉碗标本

Five Dynasties

Specimens of green glaze bowl

## 543　五代　青釉碗标本

Five Dynasties

Specimens of green glaze bowl

544　五代　青釉碗标本
Five Dynasties
Specimen of green glaze bowl

545　宋　青釉碗标本
Song dynasty
Specimen of green glaze bowl

546　**宋　青釉碗标本**

Song dynasty

Specimens of green glaze bowl

547 **宋 青釉碗标本**

Song dynasty

Specimens of green glaze bowl

548 **宋 窑具标本**
Song dynasty
Specimens of kiln furniture

# 临海窑

为一处东晋至宋代的瓷窑。2008年故宫博物院部分专家学者调查了临海鲶鱼坑口、安王山、梅浦窑。

东晋时期窑址以鲶鱼坑口窑、安王山窑为代表，烧制青釉碗、盘、罐、盘口壶、耳杯等。有非常青翠、玻璃质感很强的釉色，质量极好。有的施加褐色点彩。碗、盘采用细小的支钉支烧，工艺精湛。

唐、宋时期梅浦窑烧造青釉、黑釉器物，有碗、盘、瓶、壶、钵等，唐代有玉璧底碗，色好者与越窑相似。宋代烧造青釉瓷器，造型、釉色与越窑相似，装饰有刻划花，质量精美。

# Linhai Kiln

Linhai kiln sites were dated back from Eastern Jin dynasty to Song dynasty. Experts from the Palace Museum investigated kiln sites at Nianyukengkou, Anwangshan and Meipu in 2008.

Represented by Anwangshan and Nianyukengkou, kilns of Eastern Jin dynasty fired green glaze bowls, plates, jars, pots with dish-shaped mouth, cups, etc. Their quality is excellent for very bright green and strong glassy glaze. Some were applied with brown color design. Bowls and plates were fired using very fine supporting spurs, a-state-of-art technology.

Such green and black glaze wares as bowls, plates, vases, pots, alms bowls, etc. were fired at Meipu in Tang and Song dynasty. Bowls with jade Bi-shaped bottom and better glaze color of Tang dynasty are comparable with that of Yue kiln. Green glaze wares fired in Song dynasty are similar to those of Yue kiln in term of shaping and glaze color. They are with incised design and of excellent quality.

**临海（鲶鱼坑口）窑遗址保护牌**

Monument for protecting the ruin of Linhai kiln at Nianyukengkou

549 **东晋 青釉带系罐标本**
Eastern Jin dynasty
Specimen of green glaze jar with handles

550 **东晋 青釉双复系罐标本**
Eastern Jin dynasty
Specimen of green glaze jar with two handles

551 **东晋 青釉盘口壶标本**
Eastern Jin dynasty
Specimens of green glaze pot with dish-shaped mouth

552 东晋 青釉碗标本
Eastern Jin dynasty
Specimens of green glaze bowl

553 东晋 青釉碗标本
Eastern Jin dynasty
Specimens of green glaze bowl

554　**东晋　青釉盘标本**
Eastern Jin dynasty
Specimen of green glaze plate

555　**东晋　青釉盆标本**
Eastern Jin dynasty
Specimen of green glaze basin

556　**东晋　青釉折沿盆标本**
Eastern Jin dynasty
Specimen of green glaze basin with everted flange

557　**东晋　青釉弦纹罐标本**
Eastern Jin dynasty
Specimen of green glaze jar with strings

558　**东晋　青釉褐斑盘口壶标本**
Eastern Jin dynasty
Specimen of green glaze pot with dish-shaped mouth and brown splashes

## 559　东晋　青釉褐斑碗标本

Eastern Jin dynasty

Specimens of green glaze bowl with brown splashes

560　**东晋　青釉褐斑碗标本**

Eastern Jin dynasty

Specimens of green glaze bowl with brown splashes

561　东晋　青釉褐斑碗标本
Eastern Jin dynasty
Specimen of green glaze bowl with brown splashes

562　东晋　青釉褐斑弦纹缸标本
Eastern Jin dynasty
Specimen of green glaze vat with brown splashes and strings

**临海（安王山）窑遗址保护牌**
Monument for protecting the ruin of Linhai kiln at Anwangshan

**临海（安王山）窑遗址**
Ruin of Linhai kiln at Anwangshan

## 563　东晋　青釉碗标本

Eastern Jin dynasty

Specimens of green glaze bowl

## 564 东晋 青釉碗标本
Eastern Jin dynasty
Specimens of green glaze bowl

## 565 东晋 青釉碗标本

Eastern Jin dynasty

Specimens of green glaze bowl

566 东晋 青釉碗标本
Eastern Jin dynasty
Specimens of green glaze bowl

567 东晋 青釉弦纹钵标本
Eastern Jin dynasty
Specimen of green glaze alms bowl with strings

568 东晋 青釉褐斑壶标本
Eastern Jin dynasty
Specimen of green glaze pot with brown splashes

569 **东晋 青釉褐斑碗标本**

Eastern Jin dynasty

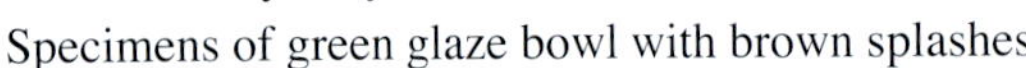

Specimens of green glaze bowl with brown splashes

570 **东晋 青釉褐斑碗标本**

Eastern Jin dynasty

Specimens of green glaze bowl with brown splashes

571 东晋 窑变釉罐标本
Eastern Jin dynasty
Specimen of flambe glaze jar

572 东晋 窑变釉碗标本
Eastern Jin dynasty
Specimen of flambe glaze bowl

573 东晋 窑具标本
Eastern Jin dynasty
Specimens of kiln furniture

574 **东晋　窑具标本**
Eastern Jin dynasty
Specimen of kiln furniture

575 **东晋　窑具标本**
Eastern Jin dynasty
Specimens of kiln furniture

**临海（梅浦）窑遗址瓷片遗存**
Pileup of porcelain parts at the ruin of Linhai kiln at Meipu

576 **宋　青釉罐标本**
Song dynasty
Specimen of green glaze jar

577 **宋　青釉罐标本**
Song dynasty
Specimens of green glaze jar

578　**宋　青釉带系罐标本**
Song dynasty
Specimens of green glaze jar with handles

579　**宋　青釉带系瓜棱罐标本**
Song dynasty
Specimen of green glaze melon-shaped jar with handles

580 **宋　青釉壶标本**
Song dynasty
Specimen of green glaze pot

581 **宋　青釉瓜棱壶标本**
Song dynasty
Specimen of green glaze melon-shaped jar

582 **宋　青釉盒标本**
Song dynasty
Specimen of green glaze box

583 宋 青釉碗标本

Song dynasty

Specimens of green glaze bowl

## 584 宋 青釉碗标本

Song dynasty

Specimens of green glaze bowl

585 宋 青釉花口碗标本

Song dynasty

Specimen of green glaze bowl with flower rim

586 宋 青釉高足碗标本

Song dynasty

Specimen of green glaze bowl with high stem

587 **宋　青釉钵标本**
Song dynasty
Specimen of green glaze alms bowl

588 **宋　青釉刻放射纹碗标本**
Song dynasty
Specimen of green glaze bowl with incised design of rays

589 宋 青釉刻放射纹碗标本

Song dynasty

Specimens of green glaze bowl with incised design of rays

590 宋 青釉刻放射纹碗标本
Song dynasty Specimen of green glaze bowl with incised design of rays

591 宋 青釉刻花莲瓣纹高足碗标本
Song dynasty Specimen of green glaze bowl with high stem and incised lotus-petal design

592　宋　黑釉碗标本
Song dynasty
Specimens of black glaze bowl

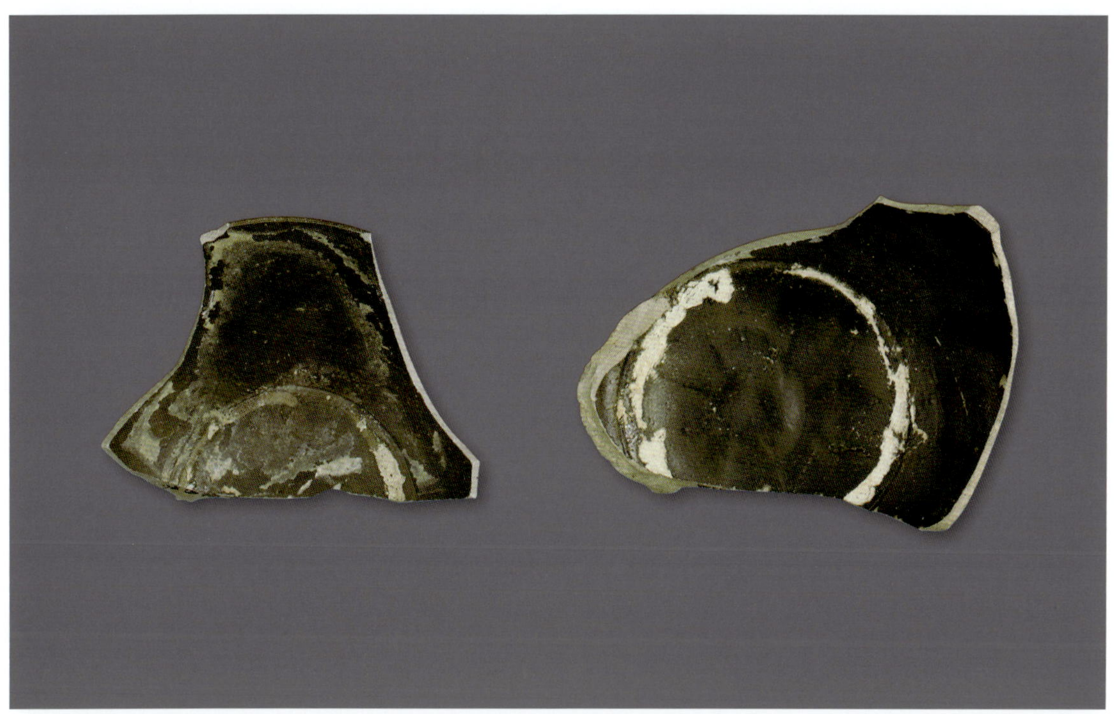

593 **宋　黑釉碗标本**
Song dynasty
Specimen of black glaze bowl

594 **宋　窑具标本**
Song dynasty
Specimen of kiln furniture

595 宋 窑具标本
Song dynasty
Specimens of kiln furniture

596 宋 窑具标本
Song dynasty
Specimens of kiln furniture

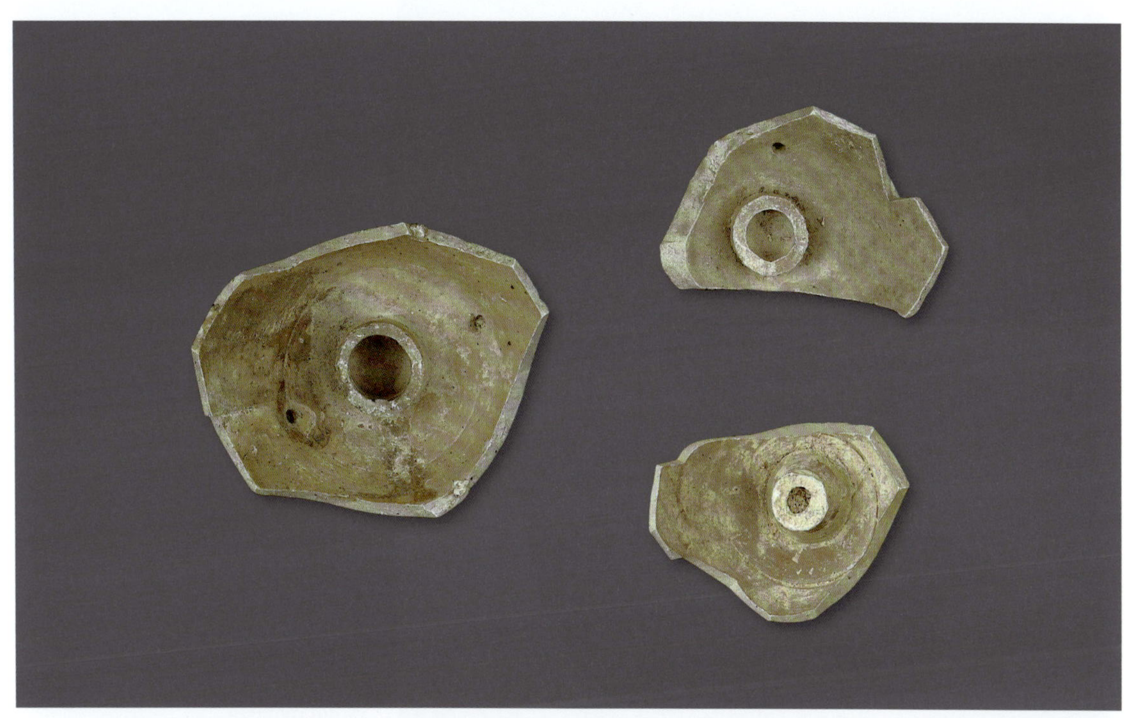

597　宋　窑具标本
Song dynasty
Specimen of kiln furniture

598　宋　窑具标本
Song dynasty
Specimen of kiln furniture

599 宋 窑具标本

Song dynasty

Specimens of kiln furniture

# 黄岩窑

窑址在浙江省黄岩县沙埠街和凤凰山一带，共有窑址八处，故宫博物院部分专家学者 20 世纪 70 年代、2008 年调查了竺家岭、凤凰山等窑址。

竺家岭窑址面积最大，所烧瓷器有精粗之分。精者有刻花鹦鹉纹的，釉色青绿，双鹦对舞，与余姚、鄞县、上虞划花鹦鹉纹风格不同；粗者以刻花篦划纹装饰居多，纹饰线条流畅生动。

# Huangyan Kiln

Huangyan kiln is located around Shabujie and Fenghuangshan, Huangyan County, Zhejiang Province. So far, eight kiln sites have been found. Experts from the Palace Museum investigated kiln sites at Zhujialing and Fenghuangshan in the 1970s and in 2008.

Zhujialing, the largest kiln site of all, fired porcelains of good and less good quality. The good ones have bright green glaze and with incised design of pair parrots in dancing, which are different from the parrots appeared on wares by Yuyao, Yinxian and Shangyu kiln. The less good ones are usually with incised design of comb patterns. The incised lines are smooth and patterns are vivid.

**黄岩窑遗址瓷片遗存**

Pileup of porcelain parts at the ruin of Huangyan kiln

600 宋 青釉碗标本
Song dynasty
Specimen of green glaze bowl

601 宋 青釉盘标本
Song dynasty
Specimen of green glaze plate

602　宋　青釉刻花花卉纹碗标本
Song dynasty
Specimen of green glaze bowl with incised floral design

603　宋　青釉刻花菊花纹碗标本
Song dynasty
Specimen of green glaze bowl with incised chrysanthemum design

## 604 宋　青釉刻花菊花纹碗标本

Song dynasty

Specimens of green glaze bowl with incised chrysanthemum design

605　宋　青釉刻线纹碗标本

Song dynasty

Specimens of green glaze bowl with incised line design

606　**宋　青釉刻线纹碗标本**

Song dynasty

Specimen of green glaze bowl with incised line design

607　**宋**

**青釉刻花篦划纹器盖标本**

Song dynasty

Specimen of green glaze cover with comb-incised design

608　宋　青釉刻花篦划印花团菊纹碗标本

Song dynasty

Specimen of green glaze bowl with comb-incised and stamped medallion of chrysanthemum design

## 609 宋 青釉刻划花花卉纹碗标本

Song dynasty

Specimens of green glaze bowl with incised floral design

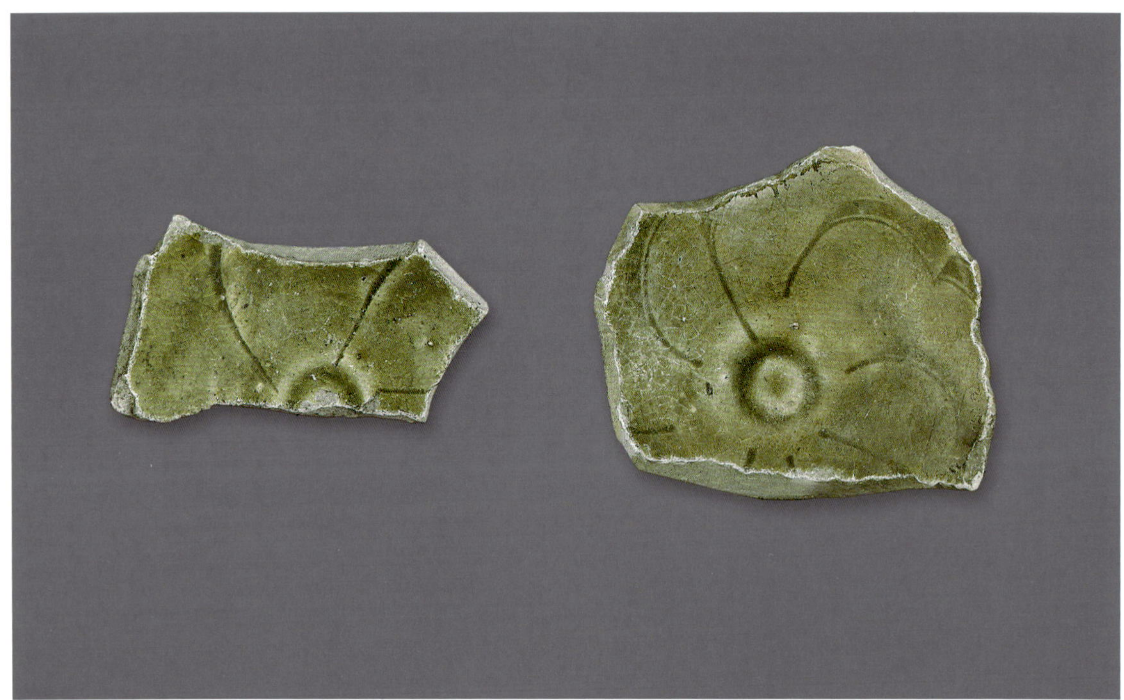

610　宋　青釉刻划花篦划纹碗标本

Song dynasty

Specimens of green glaze bowl with comb-incised design

611　**宋　青釉刻划花篦划纹碗标本**

Song dynasty

Specimens of green glaze bowl with comb-incised design

612　**宋**

**青釉刻划花篦划纹碗标本**

Song dynasty

Specimen of green glaze bowl with comb-incised design

613　**宋　青釉刻划花篦划纹碗标本**

Song dynasty

Specimen of green glaze bowl with comb-incised design

614　宋　青釉刻划花篦划纹碗标本

Song dynasty

Specimens of green glaze bowl with comb-incised design

615　宋　青釉刻划花篦划花卉纹碗标本

Song dynasty

Specimens of green glaze bowl with comb-incised floral design

616　宋　青釉里刻划花篦划印花团菊纹外刻线纹碗标本

Song dynasty

Specimens of green glaze bowl with comb-incised and stamped medallion of chrysanthemum inside and incised lines outside

617　宋　青釉里刻划花篦划印花团菊纹外刻线纹碗标本

Song dynasty

Specimens of green glaze bowl with comb-incised and stamped medallion of chrysanthemum inside and incised lines outside

618　**宋　青釉划花篦划纹碗标本**

Song dynasty

Specimens of green glaze bowl with comb-incised design

619　**宋　青釉划花篦划纹碗标本**

Song dynasty

Specimen of green glaze bowl with comb-incised design

620　**宋　青釉里划花外刻线纹碗标本**

Song dynasty

Specimen of green glaze bowl with incised design inside and incised line design outside

621　**宋　青釉里划花花瓣纹外刻线纹碗标本**

Song dynasty

Specimen of green glaze bowl with incised design of flower-petal inside and lines outside

622　宋　青釉里划花篦划纹外刻线纹碗标本
Song dynasty
Specimen of green glaze bowl with comb-incised design inside and incised line design outside

623　宋　青釉里划花篦点纹外刻线纹碗标本
Song dynasty
Specimen of green glaze bowl with comb-incised dots inside and incised line design outside

624　**宋　窑具标本**
Song dynasty
Specimens of kiln furniture

625　**宋　窑具标本**
Song dynasty
Specimen of kiln furniture

# 台州窑

2008年1月，故宫博物院部分专家学者对台州路桥地区的红沙岭、大板坦、黄家山、虎头山、红屿埠头坦、茅草山窑遗址进行了调查。

该地区烧瓷时间较早，从汉代一直到三国两晋时期。窑址较多。红沙岭窑烧青釉双系罐、盘口壶、碗、折沿盆，青釉褐斑双系罐、碗等；大板坦窑烧青釉双系罐、盘口壶、坛、钵、碗，青釉褐斑双系罐等；黄家山窑烧青釉双系罐、坛、器柄、盘口壶、罐、洗、盆、碗，青釉褐斑双系罐、碗等，双系罐系上印有纹饰；虎头山窑烧青釉双系罐，有的系为双复系，还有缸、钵、盆、碗等；茅草山窑烧青釉褐斑盘口壶、碗，青釉盆、碗等，从器物看时代多为东晋时期。

# Taizhou Kiln

Experts from the Palace Museum investigated Taizhou kiln at Hongshaling, Dabantan, Huangjiashan, Hutoushan, Hongyubutoutan and Maocaoshan in Luqiao area of Taizhou City in January, 2008.

The region started firing porcelains at a very earlier stage, from Han dynasty, Three Kingdoms to Western and Eastern Jin dynasty. Many kiln sites have been found in the region. At Hongshaling kiln site, green glaze jars with two handles (with brown splashes in some cases), pots with dish-shaped mouth, bowls (with brown splashes in some cases), basins with everted flange, etc. were fired. At Dabantan kiln site, green glaze jars with two handles (with brown splashes in some cases), pots with dish-shaped mouth, large jars, alms bowls, bowls, etc. were fired. At Huangjiashan kiln site, green glaze jars with two handles and stamped design (with brown splashes in some cases), large jars, handles of wares, pots with dish-shaped mouth, jars, washers, basins, bowls (with brown splashes in some cases), etc. were fired. At Hutoushan kiln site, green glaze jars with two handles (twin-handled in some cases), basins, vats, alms bowls, bowls, etc. were fired. At Maocaoshan kiln site, green glaze pots with dish-shaped mouth and brown splashes, basins, bowls (with brown splashes in some cases), etc. were fired. The wares themselves suggest they are mostly of Eastern Jin dynasty.

**台州（红沙岭）窑遗址**
Ruin of Taizhou kiln at Hongshaling

**台州（红沙岭）窑遗址**
Ruin of Taizhou kiln at Hongshaling

626 东晋 青釉带系罐标本
Eastern Jin dynasty
Specimen of green glaze jar with handles

627 东晋 青釉双复系罐标本
Eastern Jin dynasty
Specimen of green glaze jar with two handles

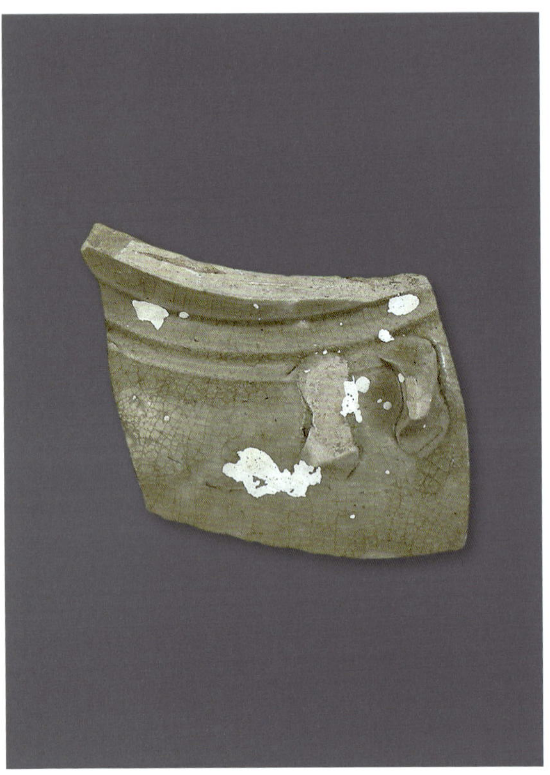

628 东晋 青釉盘口壶标本
Eastern Jin dynasty
Specimens of green glaze pot with dish-shaped mouth

629 **东晋　青釉碗标本**

Eastern Jin dynasty

Specimens of green glaze bowl

630 东晋 青釉碗标本
Eastern Jin dynasty
Specimens of green glaze bowl

631　**东晋　青釉碗标本**
Eastern Jin dynasty
Specimen of green glaze bowl

632　**东晋　青釉弦纹罐标本**
Eastern Jin dynasty
Specimen of green glaze jar
with strings

633　**东晋　青釉弦纹罐标本**
Eastern Jin dynasty
Specimens of green glaze jar with strings

634　**东晋　青釉褐斑罐标本**
Eastern Jin dynasty
Specimen of green glaze jar with brown splashes

## 635　东晋　青釉褐斑碗标本

Eastern Jin dynasty

Specimens of green glaze bowl with brown splashes

636 **东晋　青釉褐斑盆标本**
Eastern Jin dynasty　Specimen of green glaze basin with brown splashes

637 **东晋　青釉褐斑弦纹罐标本**
Eastern Jin dynasty　Specimens of green glaze jar with brown splashes and strings

638 **东晋　青釉褐斑弦纹罐标本**
Eastern Jin dynasty　Specimen of green glaze jar with brown splashes and strings

639 **东晋　青釉褐斑联珠纹罐标本**
Eastern Jin dynasty　Specimen of green glaze jar with brown splashes and pearl-bordered medallion

640 **东晋 窑具标本**

Eastern Jin dynasty

Specimens of kiln furniture

**台州（黄家山）窑遗址瓷片遗存**
Pileup of porcelain parts at the ruin of Taizhou kiln at Huangjiashan

641　东晋　青釉瓶标本
Eastern Jin dynasty
Specimens of green glaze vase

## 642　东晋　青釉带系罐标本

Eastern Jin dynasty

Specimens of green glaze jar with handles

643 **东晋 青釉带系罐标本**
Eastern Jin dynasty
Specimen of green glaze jar
with handles

644 **东晋 青釉双复系罐标本**
Eastern Jin dynasty
Specimen of green glaze jar with
two handles

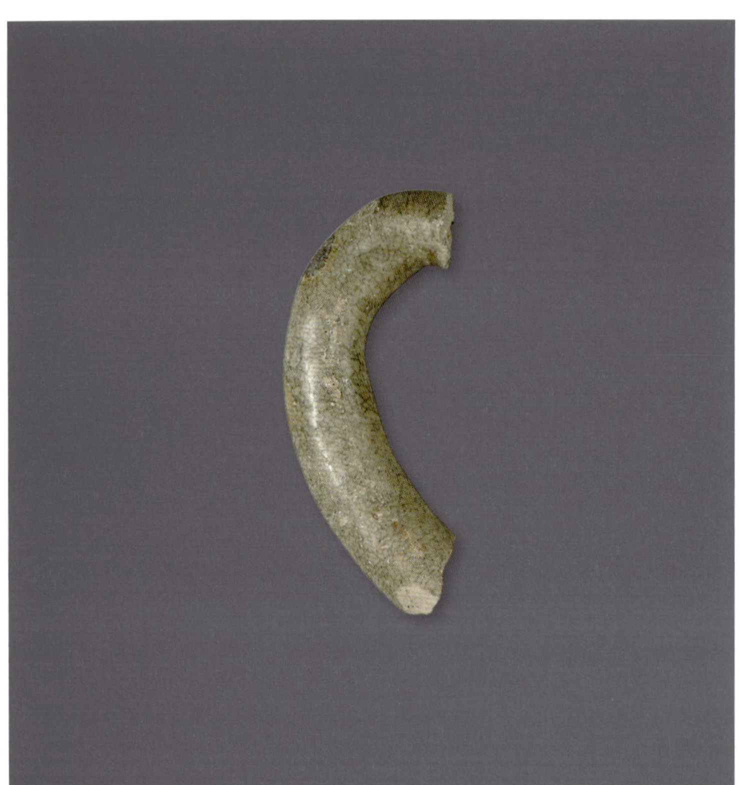

645　东晋　青釉壶标本
Eastern Jin dynasty
Specimen of green glaze pot

646　东晋　青釉坛标本
Eastern Jin dynasty
Specimens of green glaze jug

647 **东晋　青釉碗标本**
Eastern Jin dynasty
Specimens of green glaze bowl

648 **东晋　青釉碗标本**
Eastern Jin dynasty
Specimens of green glaze bowl

649　**东晋　青釉折沿洗标本**
Eastern Jin dynasty
Specimen of green glaze washer with everted flange

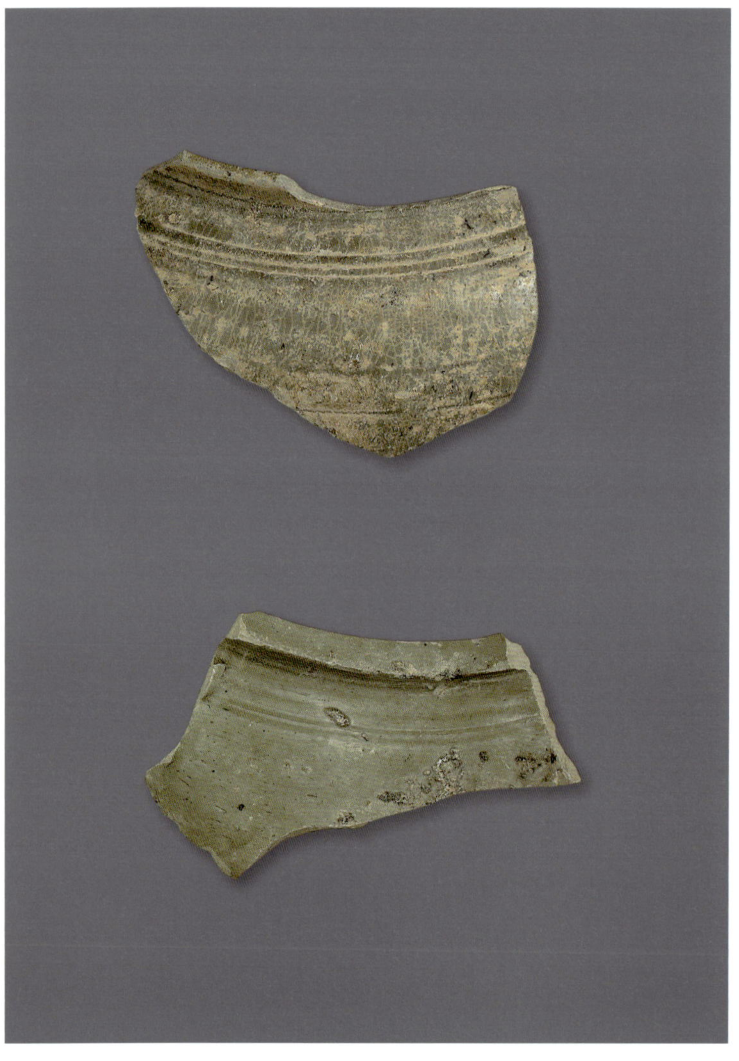

650　**东晋　青釉弦纹罐标本**
Eastern Jin dynasty
Specimens of green glaze jar with strings

651　**东晋　青釉弦纹壶标本**
Eastern Jin dynasty
Specimen of green glaze pot with strings

652　**东晋　青釉弦纹盘标本**
Eastern Jin dynasty
Specimen of green glaze plate with strings

653　**东晋　青釉弦纹钵标本**
Eastern Jin dynasty
Specimen of green glaze alms bowl with strings

654　**东晋　青釉弦纹钵标本**

Eastern Jin dynasty

Specimens of green glaze alms bowl with strings

655 **东晋　青釉弦纹钵标本**
Eastern Jin dynasty
Specimen of green glaze alms bowl with strings

656 **东晋　青釉弦纹折沿洗标本**
Eastern Jin dynasty
Specimen of green glaze washer with everted flange and strings

657　**东晋　青釉褐斑带系罐标本**

Eastern Jin dynasty

Specimens of green glaze jar with handles and brown splashes

658　**东晋　青釉褐斑盘口壶标本**

Eastern Jin dynasty

Specimen of green glaze pot with dish-shaped mouth and brown splashes

659　**东晋　青釉褐斑碗标本**

Eastern Jin dynasty

Specimens of green glaze bowl with brown splashes

660　东晋　青釉褐斑碗标本
Eastern Jin dynasty
Specimens of green glaze bowl with brown splashes

## 661 东晋 青釉褐斑弦纹罐标本

Eastern Jin dynasty

Specimens of green glaze jar with brown splashes and strings

662　东晋　窑具标本
Eastern Jin dynasty
Specimen of kiln furniture

663　东晋　窑具标本
Eastern Jin dynasty
Specimens of kiln furniture

**台州（虎头山）窑遗址**
Ruin of Taizhou kiln at Hutoushan

**台州（虎头山）窑遗址瓷片遗存**
Pieup of porcelain parts at the ruin of Taizhou kiln at Hutoushan

664　东晋　青釉带系罐标本
Eastern Jin dynasty
Specimen of green glaze jar with handles

665　东晋　青釉双复系罐标本
Eastern Jin dynasty
Specimen of green glaze jar with two handles

## 666 东晋 青釉碗标本

Eastern Jin dynasty

Specimens of green glaze bowl

667　**东晋　青釉碗标本**

Eastern Jin dynasty

Specimens of green glaze bowl

668 东晋 青釉碗标本
Eastern Jin dynasty
Specimen of green glaze bowl

669 东晋 青釉碗标本
Eastern Jin dynasty
Specimen of green glaze bowl

670 东晋 青釉钵标本
Eastern Jin dynasty
Specimen of green glaze alms bowl

671 **东晋　青釉折沿盆标本**
Eastern Jin dynasty
Specimen of green glaze basin with everted flange

672 **东晋　青釉弦纹盘口瓶标本**
Eastern Jin dynasty
Specimen of green glaze vase with dish-shaped mouth and strings

## 673 东晋 青釉弦纹盘口瓶标本

Eastern Jin dynasty Specimens of green glaze vase with dish-shaped mouth and strings

## 674 东晋 青釉弦纹洗标本

Eastern Jin dynasty

Specimens of green glaze washer with strings

675　**东晋　青釉弦纹盆标本**
Eastern Jin dynasty
Specimen of green glaze basin with strings

676　**东晋　青釉弦纹盆标本**
Eastern Jin dynasty
Specimen of green glaze basin with strings

677　**东晋　青釉弦纹盆标本**
Eastern Jin dynasty
Specimens of green glaze basin with strings

678　**东晋　青釉褐斑碗标本**

Eastern Jin dynasty

Specimens of green glaze bowl with brown splashes

## 679 东晋 青釉褐斑碗标本

Eastern Jin dynasty

Specimens of green glaze bowl with brown splashes

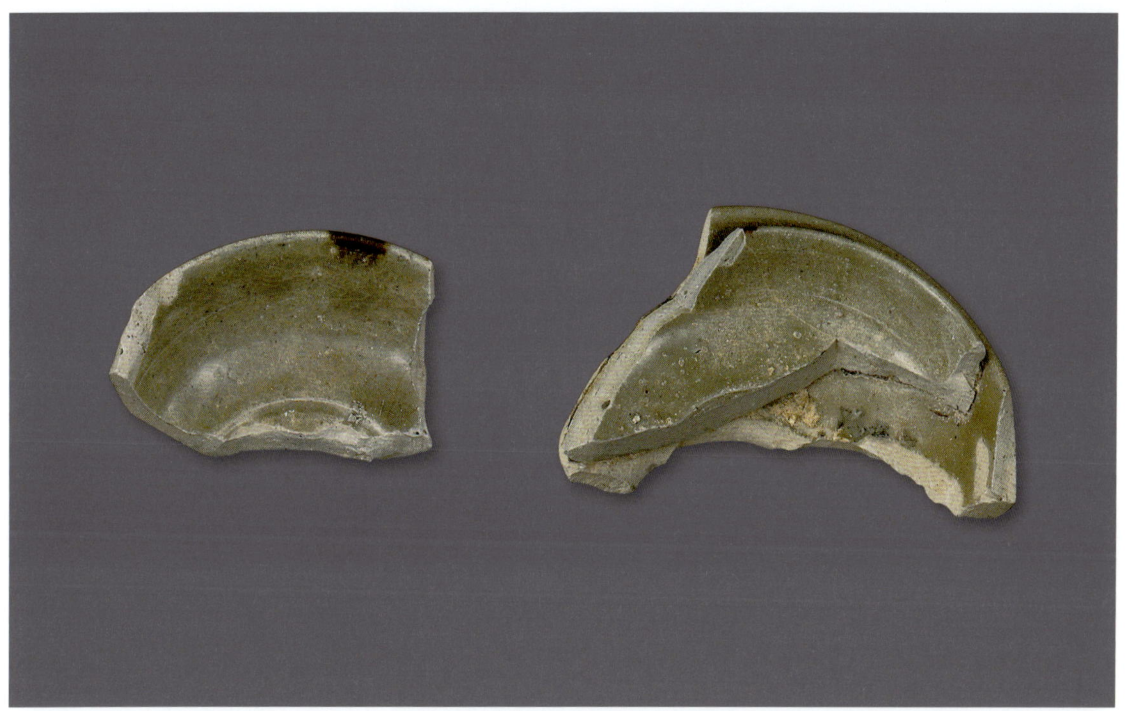

680 **东晋 青釉黑釉叠烧碗标本**
Eastern Jin dynasty
Specimen of green and black glaze bowl fired together

681 **东晋 窑具标本**
Eastern Jin dynasty
Specimen of kiln furniture

682 东晋 窑具标本
Eastern Jin dynasty
Specimens of kiln furniture

683 东晋 青釉瓶（壶）标本
Eastern Jin dynasty
Specimen of green glaze vase (pot)

684 东晋 青釉罐标本
Eastern Jin dynasty
Specimen of green glaze jar

685 **东晋 青釉双系罐标本**
Eastern Jin dynasty
Specimens of green glaze jar with two handles

686 **东晋 青釉坛标本**
Eastern Jin dynasty
Specimen of green glaze jug

687 **东晋 青釉碗标本**
Eastern Jin dynasty
Specimens of green glaze bowl

688　**东晋　青釉碗标本**

Eastern Jin dynasty

Specimens of green glaze bowl

689　**东晋　青釉钵标本**
Eastern Jin dynasty
Specimen of green glaze alms bowl

690　**东晋　青釉弦纹罐标本**
Eastern Jin dynasty
Specimen of green glaze jar with strings

691　东晋　青釉褐斑碗标本
Eastern Jin dynasty
Specimens of green glaze bowl with brown splashes

692 **东晋 窑具标本**

Eastern Jin dynasty

Specimens of kiln furniture

**台州（茅草山）窑遗址瓷片遗存**
Pileup of porcelain parts at the ruin of Taizhou kiln at Maocaoshan

**台州（茅草山）窑遗址瓷片遗存**
Pileup of porcelain parts at the ruin of Taizhou kiln at Maocaoshan

693　东晋　青釉瓶标本
Eastern Jin dynasty
Specimens of green glaze vase

694　东晋　青釉盘口壶标本
Eastern Jin dynasty
Specimen of green glaze pot with dish-shaped mouth

695 **东晋 青釉碗标本**

Eastern Jin dynasty

Specimens of green glaze bowl

696　**东晋　青釉碗标本**
Eastern Jin dynasty
Specimen of green glaze bowl

697　**东晋　青釉碗标本**
Eastern Jin dynasty
Specimens of green glaze bowl

698　东晋　青釉碗标本
Eastern Jin dynasty
Specimen of green glaze bowl

699　东晋　青釉弦纹钵缸标本
Eastern Jin dynasty
Specimen of green glaze alms bowl with strings

700　东晋　青釉褐斑罐标本
Eastern Jin dynasty
Specimen of green glaze jar with brown splashes

701　**东晋　青釉褐斑盘口壶标本**
Eastern Jin dynasty
Specimen of green glaze pot with dish-shaped mouth and brown splashes

702　**东晋　窑具标本**
Eastern Jin dynasty
Specimens of kiln furniture

# 温岭窑

2008年1月，故宫博物院部分专家学者调查了温岭下园山与老屋山窑址。

下园山窑。唐代瓷窑，产品风格与越窑极为近似。有壶、罐、瓶、碗、大钵、杯、缸、盒、花口盘、碟等，造型比较丰富。壶有瓜棱式，短颈与长颈；碗有圆式、花式、高足、玉璧底，光素与刻划花装饰；罐有双系、无系、横系、竖系，光素与划花装饰。玉璧底碗数量较多，质量较好，底有满釉与无釉者，底部留有五至七个支痕。造型、釉色与越窑非常相似，胎质细腻。唯釉色多比越窑略浅。此外还有黑釉壶、缸及花瓷拍鼓，其中花瓷拍鼓与河南鲁山窑制品很相似，但胎釉特征与制作工艺又有自身特点。是否是该窑产品，有待于进一步调查研究。窑具有各式支具、垫具。

老屋山窑。它是一处宋元时期青瓷窑址。采集的标本有青釉壶、双系罐、碗、高足碗、盘、高足盘等。碗、盘装饰很有特色，中心刻几条放射状线条，在青釉壶上饰以酱彩，青釉高足碗上涂酱色是比较特别的。器物胎釉较粗。窑具有钵形匣钵、各式垫具。

# Wenling Kiln

Experts the Palace Museum investigated Wenling kiln sites at Xiayuanshan and Laowushan of Daxi, Wenling in January, 2008.

Kiln at Xiayuanshan is a porcelain kiln of Tang dynasty. The style of its products is very similar to that of Yue kiln. It fired pots, jars, vases, bowls, cups, vats, boxes, plates with flower rim, saucers, etc. of various types. There are three kinds of pots: melon-shaped, short-necked and long-necked. Bowls can be divided into six types: round-shaped, flower-shaped, with high stem, with jade Bi-bottom, with no decoration or with incised design. Jars have the following types: with no decoration, with incised design, with two handles, no handles, horizontally or vertically arranged handles. Bowls with jade Bi-shaped bottoms (fully glazed or with no glaze), are in larger numbers and of better quality. There are 5-7 spur marks on the jade Bi-shaped bottom. Wares of Wenling kiln are very much similar to those of Yue kiln in term of shaping and glaze color. They both have very fine body. Only the glaze color of Wenling kiln wares is slightly lighter than that of Yue kiln. In addition, it fired black glaze pots, vats and speckle-glazed drums as well. Speckle-glazed drums, clearly with their own characteristics in glaze, body and firing technique, are similar to that of Lushan kiln in Henan Province. Whether speckle-glazed drums are products of Wenling kiln or not, remains a question to be further studied. Various kinds of furniture have been found at the site.

Kiln at Laowushan is a celadon kiln of Song/Yuan dynasty. Specimens collected are green glaze pots, jars with two handles, bowls, bowls with high stem, plates, plates with high stem, etc. The decoration of bowls and plates is particularly unique for the engraved several radial lines in the center. Green glaze pots with decoration of dark brown color and bowls with high stem and dark brown splashes are special, too. Wares of Kiln Laowushan are poor in glaze and body quality. Kiln furniture, such as alms bowl-shaped saggars and various kinds of pads, was found.

**温岭（下园山）窑遗址瓷片遗存**
Pileup of porcelain parts at the ruin of Wenling kiln at Xiayuanshan

**温岭（下园山）窑遗址瓷片遗存**
Pileup of porcelain parts at the ruin of Wenling kiln at Xiayuanshan

703 **唐　青釉瓜棱罐标本**
Tang dynasty
Specimen of green glaze melon-shaped jar

704 **唐　青釉双系罐标本**
Tang dynasty
Specimens of green glaze jar with two handles

705 唐 青釉双系罐标本

Tang dynasty

Specimens of green glaze jar with two handles

706 唐 青釉双系瓜棱罐标本

Tang dynasty

Specimen of green glaze melon-shaped jar with two handles

707　**唐　青釉罐（壶）标本**
Tang dynasty
Specimens of green glaze jar (pot)

708　**唐　青釉壶标本**
Tang dynasty
Specimen of green glaze pot

709　唐　青釉壶标本

Tang dynasty

Specimens of green glaze pot

## 710 唐 青釉灯标本

Tang dynasty

Specimens of green glaze lamp

711　唐　青釉盒标本
Tang dynasty
Specimen of green glaze box

712　唐　青釉碗标本
Tang dynasty
Specimen of green glaze bowl

713 **唐　青釉碗标本**

Tang dynasty

Specimens of green glaze bowl

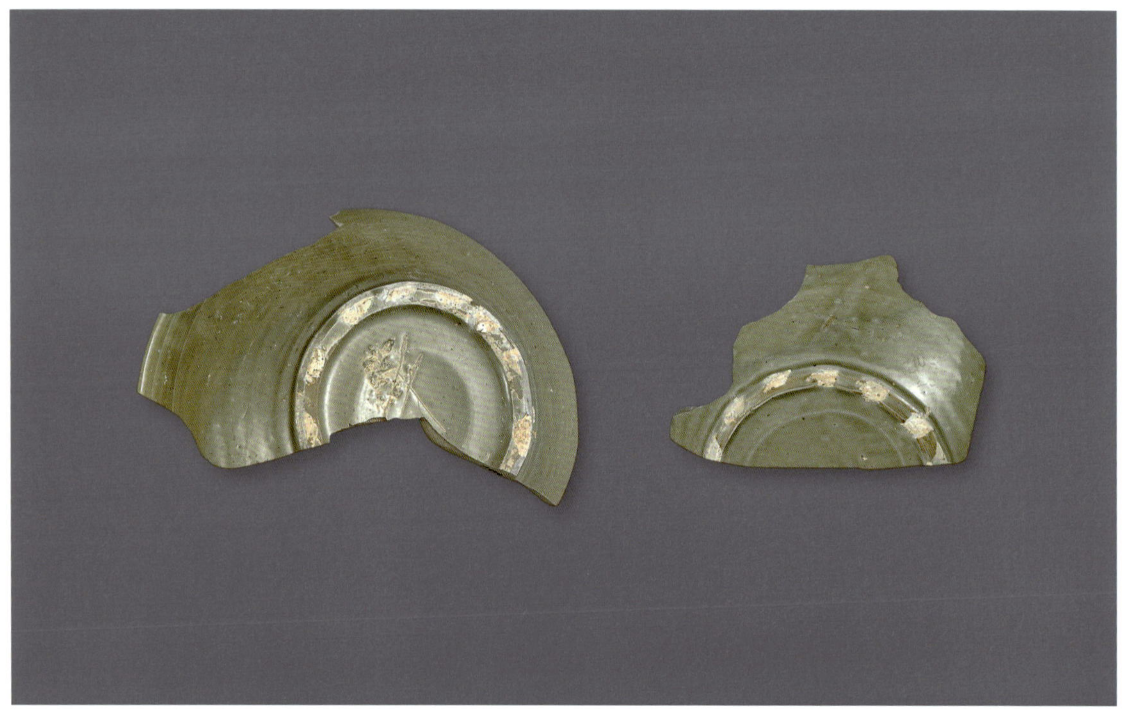

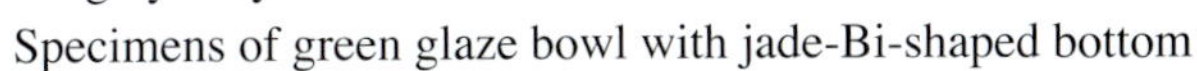
714 唐 青釉玉璧底碗标本

Tang dynasty

Specimens of green glaze bowl with jade-Bi-shaped bottom

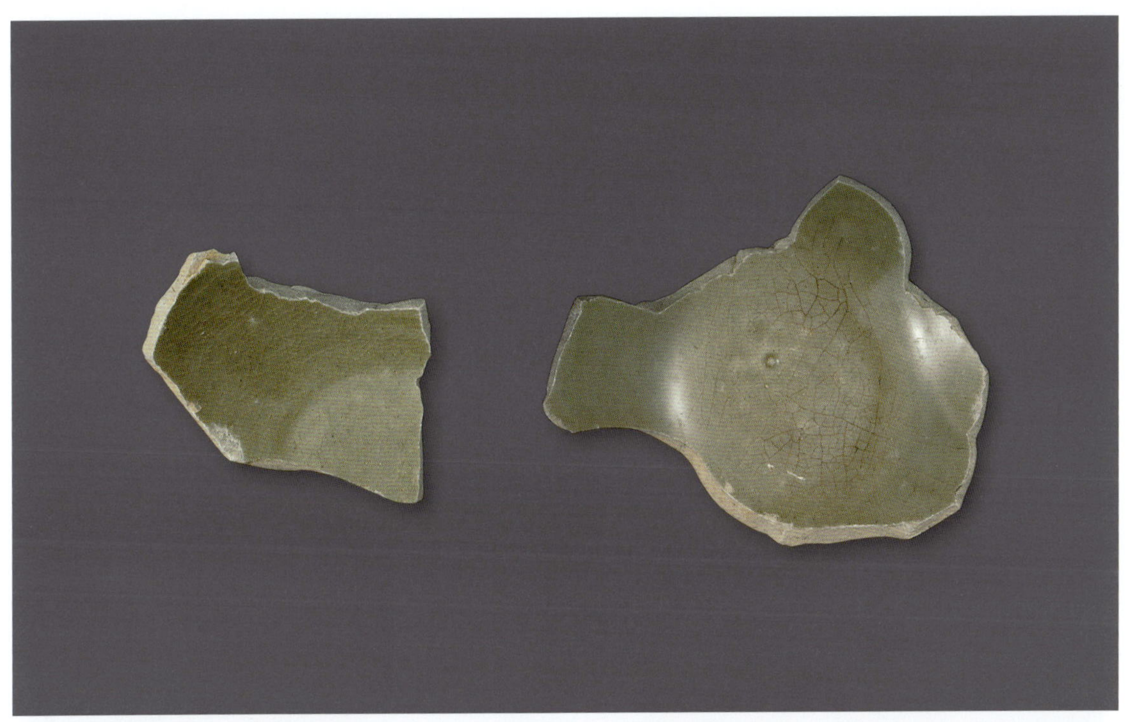

## 715 唐 青釉玉璧底碗标本

Tang dynasty

Specimens of green glaze bowl with jade-Bi-shaped bottom

716 唐 青釉钵标本

Tang dynasty

Specimen of green glaze alms bowl

717 唐 青釉钵标本

Tang dynasty

Specimen of green glaze alms bowl

718　唐　青釉钵标本
Tang dynasty
Specimens of green glaze alms bowl

719　唐　青釉盏托标本
Tang dynasty
Specimen of green glaze saucer

720 **唐　青釉杯标本**

Tang dynasty

Specimen of green glaze cup

721 **唐　青釉划花碗标本**

Tang dynasty

Specimens of green glaze bowl with incised design

722　唐　花瓷拍鼓标本
Tang dynasty
Specimen of speckle-glazed drum

723　唐　黑釉拍鼓标本
Tang dynasty
Specimen of black glaze drum

724　唐至五代　青釉花式碗标本

From Tang dynasty to Five Dynasties

Specimens of green glaze flower-shaped bowl

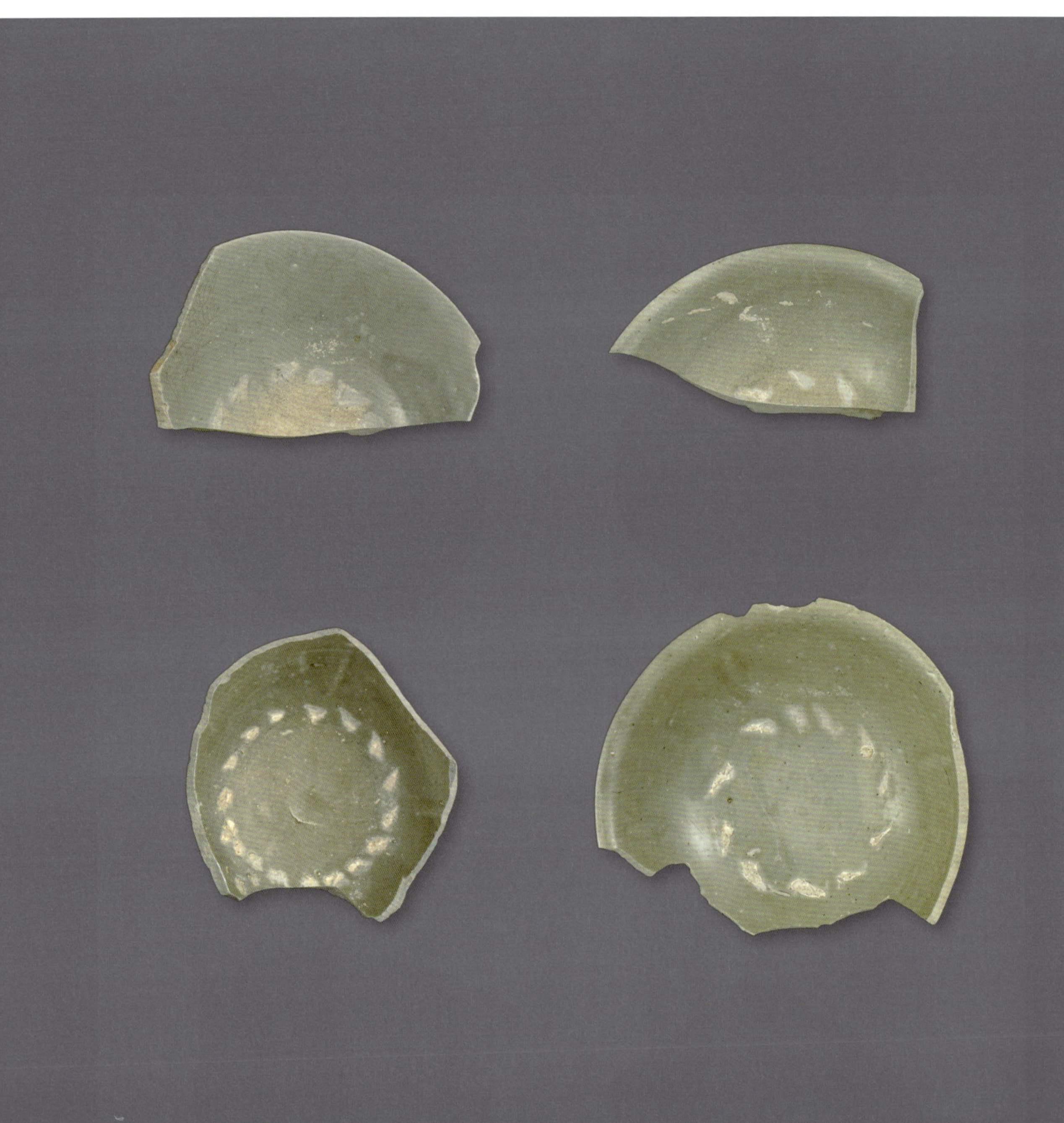

725　**五代　青釉碗标本**
Five Dynasties
Specimen of green glaze bowl

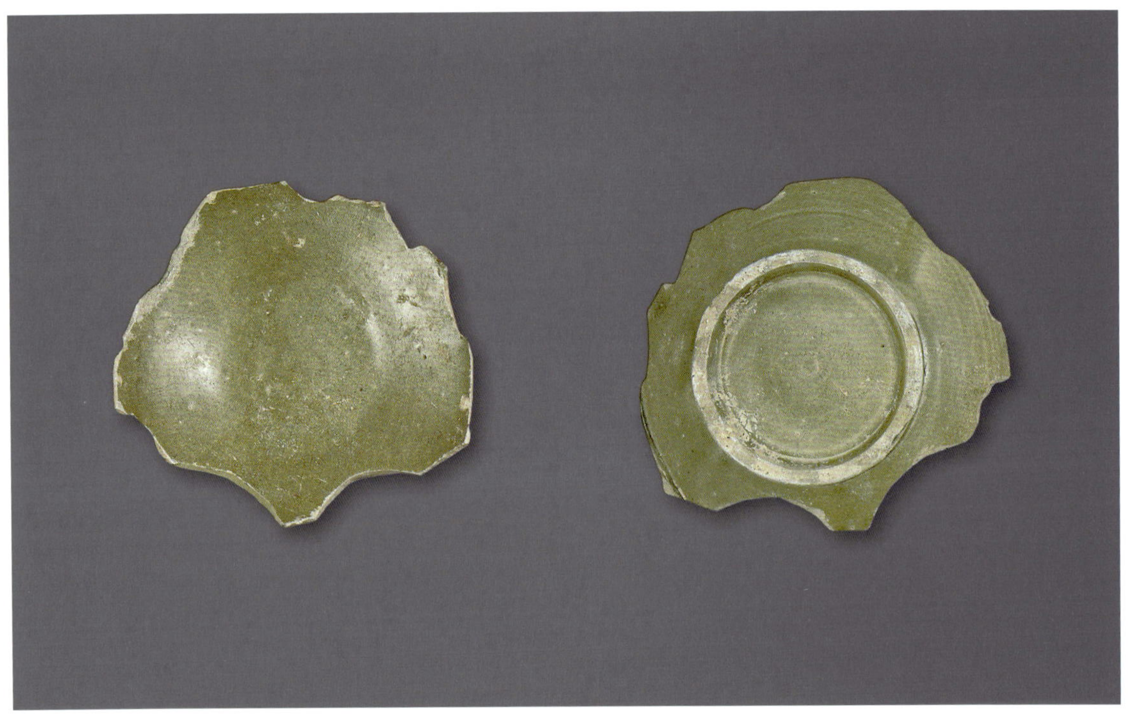

726　**五代　青釉花式碗标本**
Five Dynasties
Specimen of green glaze flower-shaped bowl

727 五代至宋 青釉花口盘标本
From Five Dynasties to Song dynasty
Specimen of green glaze plate with flower rim

728 宋
青釉刻划花篦划纹碗标本
Song dynasty
Specimen of green glaze bowl with comb-incised design

729　宋　黑釉壶标本
Song dynasty
Specimens of black glaze pot

730 **唐至宋　窑具标本**
From Tang dynasty to Song dynasty
Specimen of kiln furniture

731 **唐至宋　窑具标本**
From Tang dynasty to Song dynasty
Specimen of kiln furniture

**温岭（老屋山）窑遗址**
Ruin of Wenling kiln at Laowushan

**温岭（老屋山）窑遗址瓷片遗存**
Pileup of porcelain parts at the ruin of Wenling kiln at Laowushan

732 **宋　青釉罐标本**

Song dynasty

Specimen of green glaze jar

733　宋　青釉带系罐标本

Song dynasty

Specimen of green glaze jar with handles

734　宋　青釉壶标本

Song dynasty

Specimens of green glaze pot

735　宋　青釉碗标本

Song dynasty

Specimens of green glaze bowl

736　**宋　青釉碗标本**

Song dynasty

Specimens of green glaze bowl

737　**宋　青釉盘标本**
Song dynasty
Specimen of green glaze plate

738　**宋　青釉碟标本**
Song dynasty
Specimen of green glaze saucer

## 739　宋　青釉弦纹带系罐标本

Song dynasty

Specimens of green glaze jar with handles and strings

740　宋　青釉刻放射纹碗标本

Song dynasty

Specimens of green glaze bowl with incised design of rays

741 **宋　青釉褐彩花卉纹壶标本**

Song dynasty

Specimen of green glaze pot with design of flora in brown color

742 **宋**

**里青釉外酱釉高足器标本**

Song dynasty

Specimen of ware of green glaze inside and dark brown glaze outside with high stem

743　**宋　酱釉带系罐标本**
Song dynasty
Specimens of dark brown glaze jar
with handles

744　**宋　酱釉碗标本**
Song dynasty
Specimen of dark brown glaze bowl

# 乐清窑

窑址位于乐清市东南 20 公里虹桥镇瑶岙村碗窑山，是一处宋代窑址。2008 年 1 月故宫博物院部分专家学者调查了乐清碗窑山后山和前山窑。

该窑主要烧造青釉划花篦划纹青瓷。器类主要为碗、盘，少量瓶、罐、炉。胎质灰白，松脆。釉多青灰色，部分出现窑变。装饰有团菊纹、划花篦划纹、外刻线纹等。质量粗者，多采用刮釉支烧。

# Leqing Kiln

Leqing kiln is located at Wanyaoshan, Yaoao Village, Hongqiao Town, 20 km southeast of Leqing City. It is a Song dynasty kiln. Experts from the Palace Museum investigated Leqing kiln at Wanyaoshan in January, 2008. The kiln fired mainly green glaze wares with incised design of comb patterns, such as bowls, plates, vases, jars and burners with greyish white, soft and easily breakable body. Glaze is usually in greyish green. Some of the wares are with flambé glaze. Leqing kiln wares were decorated with medallion of chrysanthemum or incised comb patterns inside and carved double lines outside. Wares fired by supporting tools and with bottom glaze scraped away are poor in quality.

**乐清（碗窑山后山）窑遗址瓷片遗存**

Pileup of porcelain parts at the ruin of Leqing kiln at Wanyaoshanhoushan

745　**宋　青釉碗标本**

Song dynasty

Specimens of green glaze bowl

746　**宋　青釉碗标本**

Song dynasty

Specimens of green glaze bowl

747 **宋　青釉碗标本**

Song dynasty

Specimens of green glaze bowl

748　**宋　青釉花式碗标本**
Song dynasty
Specimen of green glaze flower-shaped bowl

749　**宋　青釉杯标本**
Song dynasty
Specimens of green glaze cup

## 750 宋 青釉刻线纹碗标本

Song dynasty

Specimens of green glaze bowl with incised line design

751 **宋 青釉刻线纹碗标本**

Song dynasty

Specimens of green glaze bowl with incised line design

## 752 宋 青釉刻线纹碗标本

Song dynasty

Specimens of green glaze bowl with incised line design

## 753 宋　青釉里刻划花篦划纹外刻线纹碗标本

Song dynasty

Specimens of green glaze bowl with comb-incised design  inside and incised line design outside

754　宋　青釉划花篦划纹碗标本

Song dynasty

Specimens of green glaze bowl with comb-incised design

755　宋　青釉划花篦划纹碗标本

Song dynasty

Specimens of green glaze bowl with comb-incised design

756 **宋　青釉划花篦划纹碗标本**

Song dynasty

Specimens of green glaze bowl with comb-incised design

757 **宋 黑褐釉碗标本**

Song dynasty

Specimens of blackish brown glaze bowl

乐清（碗窑山前山）窑遗址
Ruin of Leqing kiln at Wanyaoshanqianshan

758　**宋　青釉刻线纹碗标本**

Song dynasty

Specimens of green glaze bowl with incised line design

## 759　宋　青釉刻划花篦划纹碗标本

Song dynasty

Specimens of green glaze bowl with comb-incised design

760 宋 青釉划花篦划纹碗标本

Song dynasty

Specimens of green glaze bowl with comb-incised design

761 **宋 青釉划花篦划纹碗标本**

Song dynasty

Specimens of green glaze bowl with comb-incised design

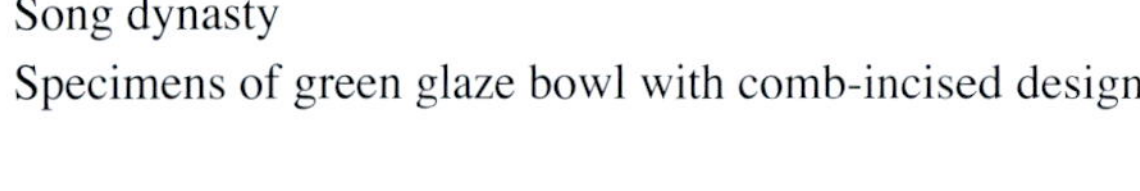

762 **宋　青釉划花篦划纹碗标本**

Song dynasty

Specimens of green glaze bowl with comb-incised design

763 宋 青釉划花篦划团菊纹碗标本
Song dynasty Specimen of green glaze bowl with comb-incised design of medallion of chrysanthemum

764 宋 窑具标本
Song dynasty
Specimens of kiln furniture

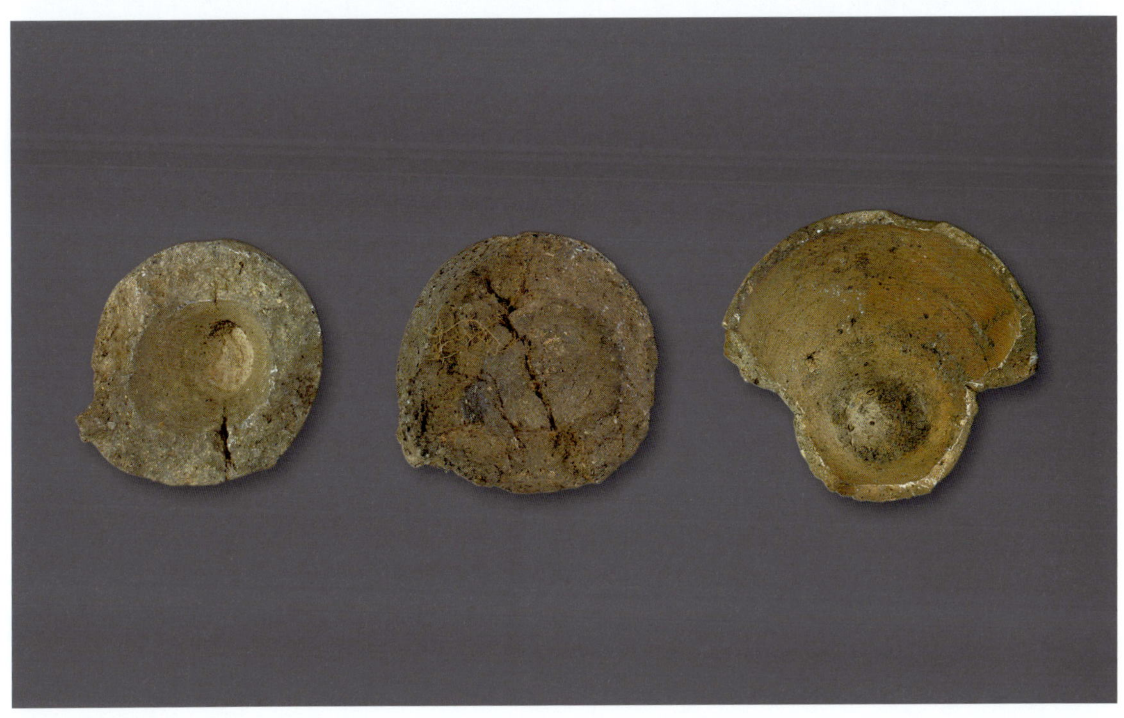

# 永嘉窑

20 世纪 50 年代、2007 年 12 月，故宫博物院部分专家学者调查了永嘉东汉时期的殿岭山窑、两晋时期的夏壁山窑、唐代的启灶窑和元明时期的钟山窑址。

永嘉地区窑址数量较多，约 50 余处，以夏壁山窑址出土物质量较好，有青釉砚、钵、盘口壶、鸡首壶等。有的施以褐彩。

启灶窑。因修铁路已遭到破坏，窑址标本散落，采集到唐至五代青釉碗、罐、钵等标本，釉色较浅，胎较厚重。

钟山窑。主要烧造龙泉窑系青釉器，有碗、盘、炉等，胎体厚重，有的饰有印花装饰，碗、盘多刮釉支烧。

# Yongjia Kiln

Experts from the Palace Museum investigated Yongjia kiln sites at Dianlingshan (dated back to Eastern Han dynasty), Xiabishan (dated back to Western and Eastern Jin dynasty), Qizao (dated back to Tang dynasty), Zhongshan (dated back to Yuan and Ming dynasty) in the 1950s and in December, 2007.

There are about 50 kiln sites found in Yongjia area. At Xiabishan kiln site, specimens of very good quality, such as green glaze ink slab, alms bowl, pot with dish-shaped mouth, chicken-spout ewer etc., were collected. Some of them are with decoration of brown color.

Owing to the construction of a railway, kiln site at Qizao was ruined. Porcelain parts were lying on the ground. Specimens collected are green glaze bowls, jars, alms bowls, etc. from Tang dynasty to Five Dynasties, whose glaze color is relatively lighter and body is relatively thicker and heavier.

Kiln at Zhongshan fired mainly Longquan kiln alike green glaze wares with thick and heavy body, such as bowls, plates, burners, etc. Some are with stamped design. For bowls and plates, they were usually fired by supporting tools and with bottom glaze scraped away.

765　**东晋　青釉器标本**
Eastern Jin dynasty
Specimen of green glaze ware

766　**东晋　青釉碗标本**
Eastern Jin dynasty
Specimens of green glaze bowl

## 767 东晋　青釉碗标本

Eastern Jin dynasty

Specimens of green glaze bowl

768 **东晋　青釉褐斑碗标本**
Eastern Jin dynasty
Specimen of green glaze bowl with brown splashes

769 **东晋　窑具标本**
Eastern Jin dynasty
Specimen of kiln furniture

770 **东晋　窑具标本**
Eastern Jin dynasty
Specimens of kiln furniture

永嘉（启灶）窑遗址

Ruin of Yongjia kiln at Qizao

771　**唐至五代　青釉壶（罐）标本**

From Tang dynasty to Five Dynasties

Specimens of green glaze pot (jar)

772　唐至五代　青釉碗标本

From Tang dynasty to Five Dynasties

Specimens of green glaze bowl

773 **唐至五代　青釉碗标本**

From Tang dynasty to Five Dynasties

Specimens of green glaze bowl

774 **唐至五代 青釉盘标本**
From Tang dynasty to Five Dynasties
Specimen of green glaze plate

775 **唐至五代 青釉弦纹罐标本**
From Tang dynasty to Five Dynasties
Specimen of green glaze jar with design of strings

776 **唐至五代 窑具标本**

From Tang dynasty to Five Dynasties

Specimens of kiln furniture

**永嘉（钟山）窑遗址瓷片遗存**
Pileup of porcelain parts at the ruin of Yongjia kiln at Zhongshan

777　元　青釉炉标本
Yuan dynasty
Specimen of green glaze burner

778　元　青釉碗标本
Yuan dynasty
Specimen of green glaze bowl

779　元　青釉碗标本

Yuan dynasty

Specimens of green glaze bowl

780　元　青釉碗标本
Yuan dynasty
Specimens of green glaze bowl

781　元　青釉盘标本

Yuan dynasty

Specimens of green glaze plate

782　元　青釉高足杯标本

Yuan dynasty

Specimens of green glaze cup with high stem

783　**元　青釉弦纹炉标本**
Yuan dynasty
Specimen of green glaze burner with strings

784　**元　青釉印花花卉纹碗标本**
Yuan dynasty
Specimen of green glaze bowl with stamped floral design

785　元　**青釉印花花卉纹碗标本**

Yuan dynasty

Specimens of green glaze bowl with stamped floral design

786　元　**青釉印花花卉纹碗标本**

Yuan dynasty

Specimens of green glaze bowl with stamped floral design

787　元　青釉印花花卉纹碗标本

Yuan dynasty　Specimen of green glaze bowl with stamped floral design

788　元　青釉印花花卉纹盘标本

Yuan dynasty　Specimen of green glaze plate with stamped floral design

## 789　元　青釉印花花卉纹盘标本

Yuan dynasty

Specimens of green glaze plate with stamped floral design

790　元　窑具标本
Yuan dynasty
Specimens of kiln furniture

791　元　窑具标本
Yuan dynasty
Specimen of kiln furniture

# 温州窑

窑址在浙江省温州市西山一带，面积较大，故宫博物院部分专家学者 20 世纪 50 年代、70 年代调查了此窑。

窑址目前已遭破坏，不能看到原貌。窑址采集的标本有与越窑划花风格近似的厚胎大碗，支烧方法与越窑具有共同风格。此外有执壶、盏托等。宋代标本有各式碗，里有刻花、划花装饰。执壶亦与越窑系瓷窑相似。其中一种执壶造型修长，具有该窑特点，四瓣瓜棱式执壶还保留有唐代遗风；另一种与慈溪窑的执壶相似，壶腹饰有凸棱线装饰。

温州窑器物的釉色较越窑系青瓷为浅，保留了早期缥瓷的固有传统。对温州窑的烧瓷时间目前学界尚有分歧，根据遗物的造型、纹饰分析，其时代定为晚唐至宋初比较适宜。

# Wenzhou Kiln

Wenzhou kiln is located in Xishan area, Wenzhou City, Zhejiang Province. The kiln site is quite large. Experts from the Palace Museum investigated it in the 1950s and 1970s.

Currently, the kiln site has been damaged. It is impossible to see the original state. Among the specimens collected, there is a kind of large size bowl with thick body which is very close to that of Yue kiln and so is the firing method. Other products are pots with handle at the side, saucers, etc. Specimens of Song dynasty include various bowls with incised or carved design inside. The pot with handle at the side is similar to that of Yue kiln, too. Pot with handle at the side and of slender shaping is a characteristic of Wenzhou kiln. Melon-shaped pot with handle at the side still keeps the pot-making legacy of Tang dynasty. Pot with abdomen decorated with ribs is very close to that of Cixi kiln.

The glaze color of Wenzhou kiln ware is lighter than that of Yue kiln. The former keeps porcelain-making tradition well. Arguments on when Wenzhou kiln started to fire still remain academically. Based on the shaping and decoration of relics found at the site, it is reasonable to date the kiln of late Tang to early Song dynasty.

792　晚唐　青釉花式碗标本

Late Tang dynasty

Specimen of green glaze flower-shaped bowl

793 **晚唐至五代　青釉瓜棱壶标本**

From Late Tang dynasty to Five Dynasties

Specimen of green glaze melon-shaped pot

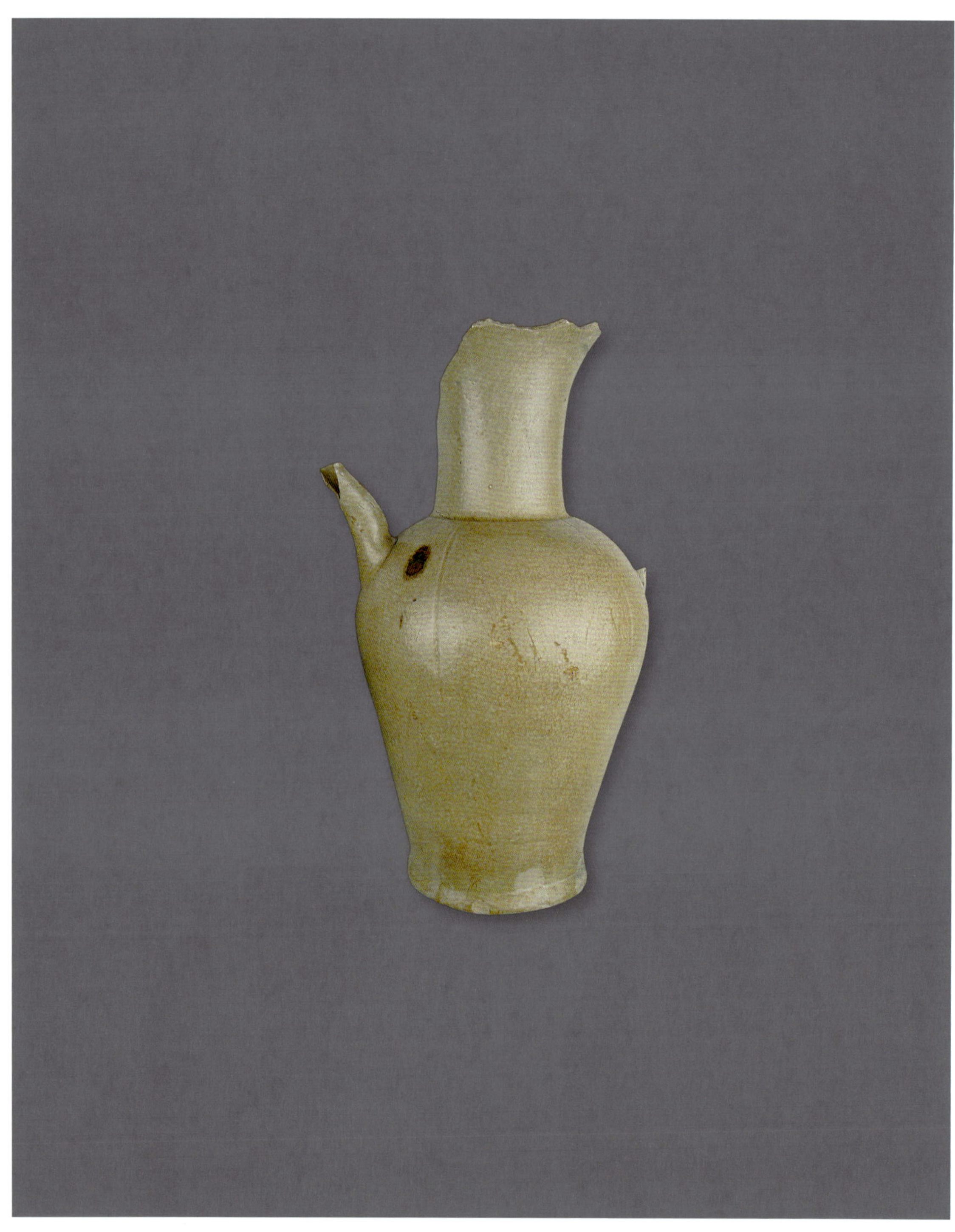

794 **晚唐至五代 青釉瓜棱双系壶标本**
From Late Tang dynasty to Five Dynasties
Specimens of green glaze melon-shaped pot with two handles

795 五代 青釉花式碗标本

Five Dynasties

Specimens of green glaze flower-shaped bowl

796　五代　青釉刻花莲瓣纹碗标本
Five Dynasties
Specimens of green glaze bowl with incised lotus-petal design

797　五代至宋
青釉刻花莲花纹碗标本
From Five Dynasties to Song dynasty
Specimen of green glaze bowl with
incised lotus design

798　**宋　青釉壶标本**

Song dynasty

Specimens of green glaze pot

附图

## 北宋　青釉褐彩蕨草纹壶

通高 25.1 厘米　口径 5.1 厘米
底径 7.5 厘米
浙江省温州市郊锦山出土

Illustration
Northern Song dynasty
Green glaze pot with design of fern in brown

Overall height 25.1cm, mouth diameter 5.1cm,
bottom diameter 7.5cm
Unearthed at Jinshan, suburb of Wenzhou City, Zhejiang Province

壶直口，长颈，丰肩，瓜棱腹，平底稍内凹，底缘外侈。肩部一侧置弧形长流，另一侧颈腹间置曲折的扁条形柄。盖为塔式，宝珠钮。灰白色胎，胎体薄，质地细腻。通体施淡青绿釉，釉面匀净。全器上下饰釉下褐彩纹饰，盖面绘草叶纹，肩腹部绘蕨草纹，色彩浓淡相宜。柄面模印缠枝花纹，其间有阳文“七何”两字。为浙江瓯窑烧造。

瓯窑是温州一带的古瓷窑，所产青釉从汉代一直延续到宋、元。青釉特点有别于越窑产品，胎质不如越窑致密，胎较白，未完全烧结，有剥釉现象。器形种类与越窑大致相同，有罐、碗、钵、洗、壶、盘等。

799 **宋　青釉瓜棱壶标本**
Song dynasty
Specimen of green glaze melon-shaped pot

800 **宋　青釉碗标本**
Song dynasty
Specimen of green glaze bowl

801　宋　青釉碗标本
Song dynasty
Specimen of green glaze bowl

802　宋　青釉碗标本
Song dynasty
Specimen of green glaze bowl

803　**宋　青釉碗标本**
Song dynasty
Specimen of green glaze bowl

804　**宋　青釉花口碗标本**
Song dynasty
Specimen of green glaze bowl
with flower rim

805 **宋 青釉盏托标本**
Song dynasty
Specimen of green glaze saucer

806 **宋 青釉盘标本**
Song dynasty
Specimen of green glaze plate

807　**宋　青釉刻花莲瓣纹碗标本**

Song dynasty

Specimen of green glaze bowl with incised lotus-petal design

808 宋 青釉刻花莲瓣叶纹碗标本
Song dynasty
Specimen of green glaze bowl with incised lotus-petal and leaf design

809 宋 青釉刻花菊花纹碗标本
Song dynasty
Specimen of green glaze bowl with incised chrysanthemum design

810 宋 青釉刻线纹碗标本
Song dynasty
Specimen of green glaze bowl with incised line design

# 瑞安窑

瑞安在浙江省南端，2007 年故宫博物院部分专家学者调查了瑞安窑的上瓷、外三甲窑址。

上瓷窑。窑址分布在瑞安市陶山镇寺前村后山坡上。从窑址标本来看，其烧瓷时间在宋元之间，主要烧制青釉器物。釉色有青灰、青绿等，器类有瓶、罐、碗、钵等，装饰团花、水波、卷草等纹饰。

外三甲窑。此窑也烧制青釉器物，器类有碗、杯、瓶、壶等。装饰分为光素及划花两类，瓶、壶类有的饰凸线纹装饰；碗内所饰细线划花，有与越窑风格接近者，也有里划花篦划纹外刻线纹者。

# Ruian Kiln

Ruian is located in the southern tip of Zhejiang Province. Experts from the Palace Museum investigated Ruian kiln at Shangciyao and Waisanjia in 2007.

Shangciyao kiln site is distributed along a slope by Siqiancun Village, Taoshan Town, Ruian City. Specimens collected from the site suggest it started to fire in between Song and Yuan dynasty. It fired mainly green glaze wares, such as vases, jars, bowls, alms bowls, etc. The glaze is in greyish green and bright green, etc. Decorative patterns are medallion, wave, grass scrolls and so on.

Green glaze wares, such as bowls, cups, vases, pots, etc., were also fired at Waisanjia kiln site. Some are without decoration and some with incised design. For vases and pots, they are decorated with lines in relief. Bowls with incised design of fine lines inside are very close to the style of Yue kiln. There are also bowls with incised design of comb patterns inside and carved double lines outside.

811　**宋　青釉瓜棱瓶标本**

Song dynasty

Specimen of green glaze melon-shaped vase

812 **宋 青釉瓜棱瓶（壶）标本**

Song dynasty

Specimens of green glaze melon-shaped vase (pot)

813　**宋　青釉瓜棱瓶（壶）标本**
Song dynasty
Specimen of green glaze melon-shaped vase (pot)

814　**宋　青釉碗标本**
Song dynasty
Specimen of green glaze bowl

## 815　宋　青釉碗标本

Song dynasty

Specimens of green glaze bowl

816 **宋　青釉碗标本**
Song dynasty
Specimens of green glaze bowl

817 **宋　青釉碗标本**
Song dynasty
Specimen of green glaze bowl

818 **宋　青釉折沿碗标本**
Song dynasty
Specimen of green glaze bowl with everted flange

819 宋 青釉刻花花卉纹碗标本

Song dynasty

Specimens of green glaze bowl with incised floral design

820 **宋　青釉刻划放射纹碗标本**

Song dynasty

Specimen of green glaze bowl with incised design of rays

821 **宋 青釉划花花叶纹碗标本**

Song dynasty

Specimens of green glaze bowl with incised flower and leaf design

822　**宋　青釉划花花叶纹碗标本**

Song dynasty

Specimen of green glaze bowl with incised flower and leaf design

823　**宋　青釉划花篦划纹碗标本**

Song dynasty

Specimen of green glaze bowl with comb-incised design

824　宋　青釉里划花花叶纹外刻线纹碗标本
Song dynasty
Specimen of green glaze bowl with incised flower and leaf design inside and incised line design outside

825　宋　窑具标本
Song dynasty
Specimens of kiln furniture

# 苍南窑

2007 年故宫博物院部分专家学者调查了苍南圣陶龙头山等窑址群，主要有龙头山、源美内、碗窑村、大脚岭等窑址。

苍南窑唐宋时期烧造瓷器。唐代烧造平底、玉璧底、假圈足碗；宋代烧造有似越窑风格的青釉瓜棱壶、浅碗、盘等。其中有划花篦划纹碗、盘，造型、胎釉与越窑青瓷极为相似。还有少量酱釉罐等。其中碗窑村窑以烧造青白釉为主，有碗、炉等，有些碗里心装饰划花篦划纹，外刻线纹，与青瓷同类装饰相似。

# Cangnan Kiln

Experts from the Palace Museum investigated Cangnan kiln sites in groups at Longtoushan, Yuanmeinei, Wanyaocun, Dajiaoling, etc. in 2007.

Cangnan kiln started firing in Tang and Song dynasty. Bowls with flat bottom, Bi-shaped bottom or false ring foot were fired in Tang dynasty. Those collected, Yue kiln alike, green glaze melon-shaped pots, shallow bowls, plates, etc. are from Song dynasty. Bowls and plates with incised design of comb patterns are very much similar to that of Yue kiln in term of shaping, glaze and body. In addition, the kiln fired a small number of dark reddish brown wares.

At Wanyaocun site, bluish white glaze wares, such as bowls, burners, etc. were fired mainly. Bluish white glaze bowls share the same decoration with green glaze ones, i.e. incised design of comb patterns inside the center and carved double lines outside.

**苍南（龙头山）窑遗址**
Ruin of Cangnan kiln at Longtoushan

826　五代至宋　青釉瓜棱壶标本
From Five Dynasties to Song dynasty
Specimen of green glaze melon-shaped pot

827 **五代至宋 青釉碗标本**

From Five Dynasties to Song dynasty

Specimens of green glaze bowl

828 **宋 青釉壶标本**

Song dynasty

Specimens of green glaze pot

829 宋 青釉壶标本
Song dynasty
Specimens of green glaze pot

830　**宋　青釉碗标本**

Song dynasty

Specimens of green glaze bowl

831　**宋　青釉碗标本**

Song dynasty

Specimens of green glaze bowl

832 **宋　青釉碗标本**

Song dynasty

Specimens of green glaze bowl

## 833 宋 青釉刻放射纹碗标本

Song dynasty

Specimens of green glaze bowl with incised design of rays

834 **宋　酱釉四系罐标本**

Song dynasty

Specimen of dark brown glaze jar with four handles

835 **五代至宋　青釉碗标本**

From Five Dynasties to Song dynasty

Specimens of green glaze bowl

836　五代至宋　青釉碗标本

From Five Dynasties to Song dynasty

Specimens of green glaze bowl

837 **五代至宋 青釉刻放射纹碗标本**

From Five Dynasties to Song dynasty

Specimens of green glaze bowl with incised design of rays

838 **宋　青釉瓶标本**
Song dynasty
Specimen of green glaze vase

839 **宋　青釉盘标本**
Song dynasty
Specimen of green glaze plate

840 **宋 窑具标本**
Song dynasty
Specimen of kiln furniture

841 **宋 窑具标本**
Song dynasty
Specimen of kiln furniture

842 **宋　青白釉罐标本**
Song dynasty
Specimen of bluish white glaze jar

843 **宋　青白釉碗标本**
Song dynasty
Specimen of bluish white glaze bowl

844 **宋　青白釉碗标本**
Song dynasty
Specimens of bluish white glaze bowl

845 宋　青白釉碗标本
Song dynasty
Specimen of bluish white glaze bowl

846 宋　青白釉折腰盘标本
Song dynasty
Specimen of bluish white glaze waisted plate

## 847 宋 青白釉划花篦划纹碗标本

Song dynasty

Specimens of bluish white glaze bowl with comb-incised design

848 **宋 青白釉里划花篦划纹外刻线纹碗标本**
Song dynasty
Specimen of bluish white glaze bowl with comb-incised design inside and incised lines outside

849 **宋 窑具标本**
Song dynasty
Specimen of kiln furniture

850 **五代至宋　青釉碗标本**

From Five Dynasties to Song dynasty

Specimens of green glaze bowl

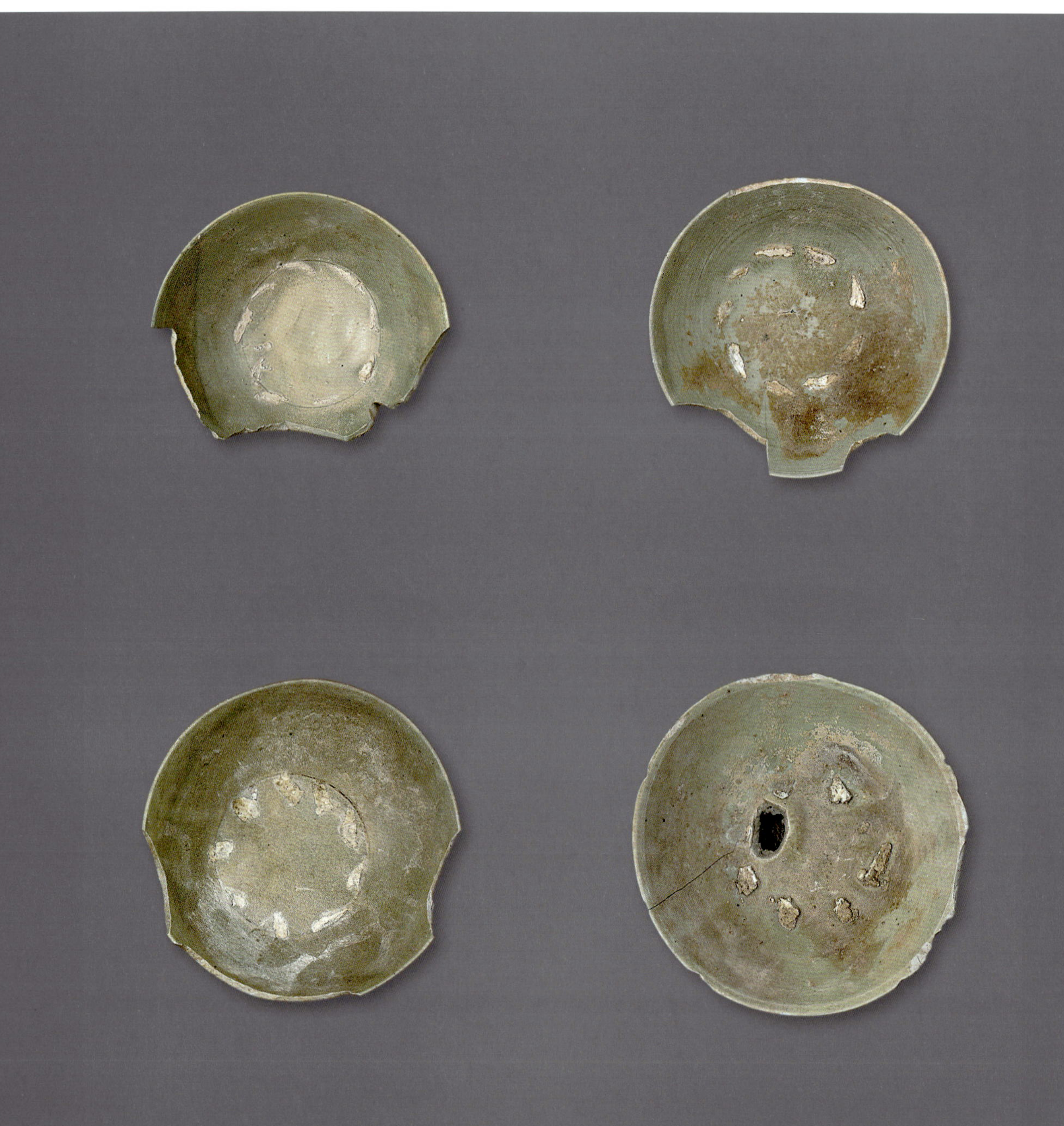

## 851　五代至宋　青釉碗标本

From Five Dynasties to Song dynasty

Specimens of green glaze bowl

852　五代至宋　青釉碗标本

From Five Dynasties to Song dynasty

Specimens of green glaze bowl

853　**宋　青釉双系瓶标本**
Song dynasty
Specimen of green glaze vase with two handles

854　**宋　青釉碗标本**
Song dynasty
Specimen of green glaze bowl

855 **宋　青釉碗标本**

Song dynasty

Specimens of green glaze bowl

856　**宋　青釉刻放射纹碗标本**

Song dynasty

Specimens of green glaze bowl with incised design of rays

857 **宋 青釉刻放射纹碗标本**

Song dynasty

Specimens of green glaze bowl with incised design of rays

858　**宋　褐釉双系罐标本**
Song dynasty
Specimen of brown glaze jar with two handles

859　**宋　窑具标本**
Song dynasty
Specimens of kiln furniture

860 **宋 窑具标本**

Song dynasty

Specimens of kiln furniture

# 泰顺窑

泰顺在浙江省最南端，窑址分布在泰顺百丈镇水库边的几座小山包上。故宫博物院部分专家学者 2007 年调查了泰顺窑背窑。

窑背窑遗址有大量窑具及瓷片堆积。该窑主要烧制青釉、青釉划花、黑褐釉瓷器。青釉碗，有的与龙泉风格近似，胎厚重，有刻划花装饰，内壁有分格纹，也有光素的。足宽浅平切，四点支烧，有的有火石红色。盘有菊瓣形的。黑釉质量较好，釉质匀净。

从故宫博物院藏调查标本可知，泰顺玉塔窑还烧制青白釉器物，器类有壶、罐、炉、灯、碗、盘、碟、盏、水盂等。碗、盘多装饰划花。

# Taishun Kiln

Taishun is in the southernmost of Zhejiang Province. Kiln sites are distributed on several hills by a reservoir in Baizhang Town. Experts from the Palace Museum investigated kiln site at Yaobeiyao in 2007.

A great many kiln furniture and porcelain parts were piled up at Yaobeiyao. The kiln mainly fired green glaze, green glaze with incised design, dark brown glaze wares. Green glaze wares are principally bowls. Those with thick and heavy body, with incised or carved design, with or without plaid patterns along inner wall, are similar to Longquan kiln style. The bowl was supported by four spurs against the bottom and fired. The foot of the bowl is wide and slightly and horizontally cut off and sometime part of it in flint red. Some plates are chrysanthemum-shaped. Black glaze wares are good quality for pure and even glaze.

Specimens collected indicate that Taishun kiln also fired bluish white glaze wares, such as pots, jars, burners, lamps, bowls, plates, dishes, saucers, water containers, etc. For bowls and plates, they are usually with incised design.

**泰顺（窑背）窑遗址**
Ruin of Taishun kiln at Yaobei

861 唐 青釉玉璧底碗标本
Tang dynasty
Specimen of green glaze bowl with foot in shape of jade Bi

862 五代至宋 黑釉碗标本
From Five Dynasties to Song dynasty
Specimen of black glaze bowl

863 五代至宋 黑釉碗标本
From Five Dynasties to Song dynasty
Specimen of black glaze bowl

864 南宋 黑釉碗标本
Southern Song dynasty
Specimen of black glaze bowl

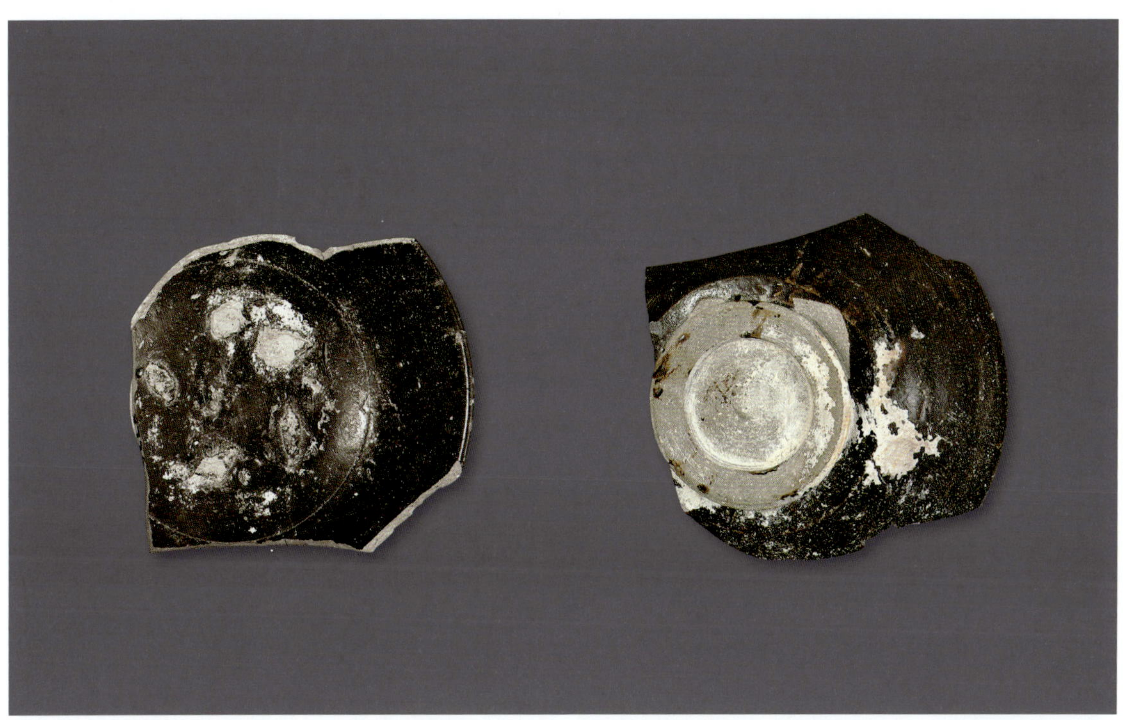

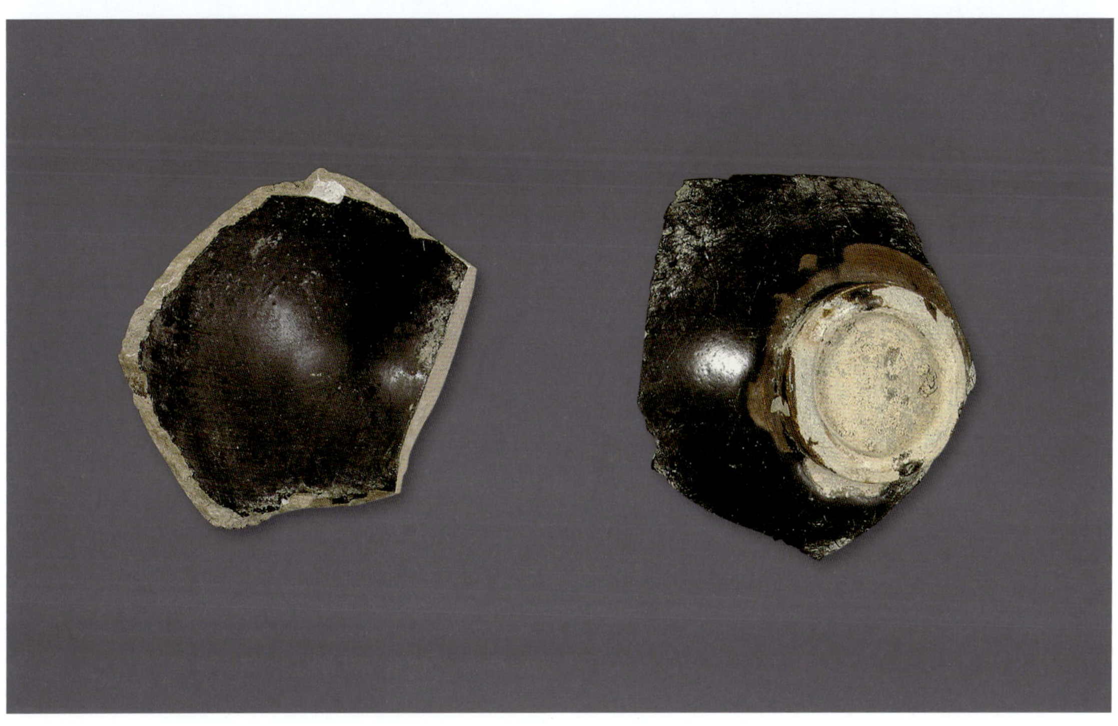

865　**南宋　黑釉碗标本**

Southern Song dynasty

Specimens of black glaze bowl

866　**南宋　黑釉碗标本**

Southern Song dynasty

Specimen of black glaze bowl

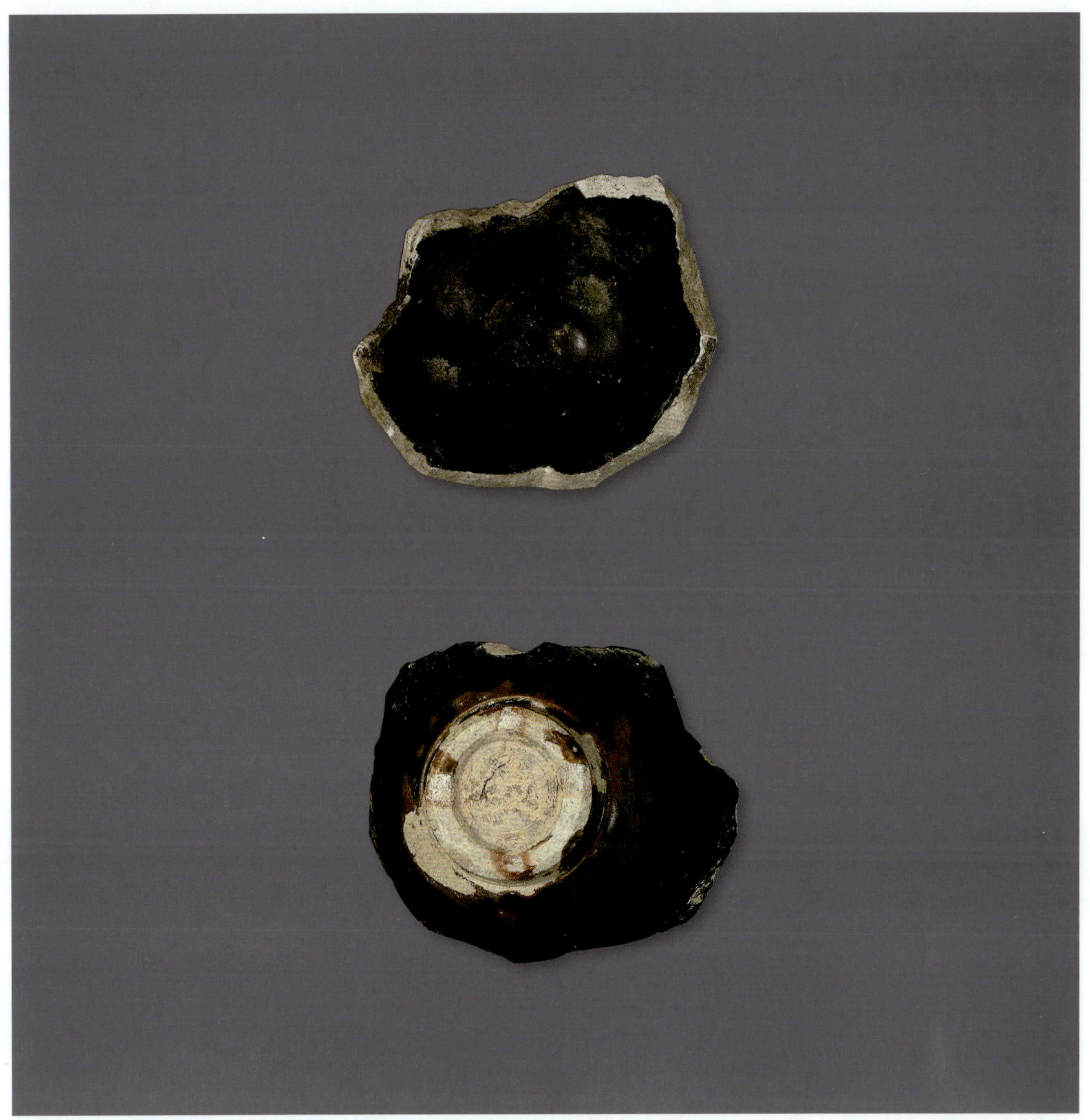

867　**南宋至元　青釉碗标本**

From Southern Song dynasty to Yuan dynasty

Specimens of green glaze bowl

868 南宋至元 青釉碗标本
From Southern Song dynasty to Yuan dynasty
Specimens of green glaze bowl

869 **南宋至元　青釉碗标本**

From Southern Song dynasty to Yuan dynasty

Specimens of green glaze bowl

870　**南宋至元　青釉刻分格纹碗标本**

From Southern Song dynasty to Yuan dynasty

Specimens of green glaze bowl with incised design of panels

871 **南宋至元　青釉刻分格纹碗标本**

From Southern Song dynasty to Yuan dynasty

Specimen of green glaze bowl with incised design of panels

872 南宋至元 青釉刻划花荷莲纹碗标本
From Southern Song dynasty to Yuan dynasty
Specimens of green glaze bowl with incised lotus design

873 **南宋至元　青釉刻划花荷莲纹碗标本**

From Southern Song dynasty to Yuan dynasty

Specimen of green glaze bowl with incised lotus design

874　南宋至元　青釉刻划花篦划纹碗标本
From Southern Song dynasty to Yuan dynasty
Specimens of green glaze bowl with comb-incised design

## 875　南宋至元　青釉刻划花篦划纹碗标本

From Southern Song dynasty to Yuan dynasty

Specimens of green glaze bowl with comb-incised design

876　**南宋至元　青釉黑釉叠烧碗标本**

From Southern Song dynasty to Yuan dynasty

Specimens of black glaze bowl and green glaze bowl fired together

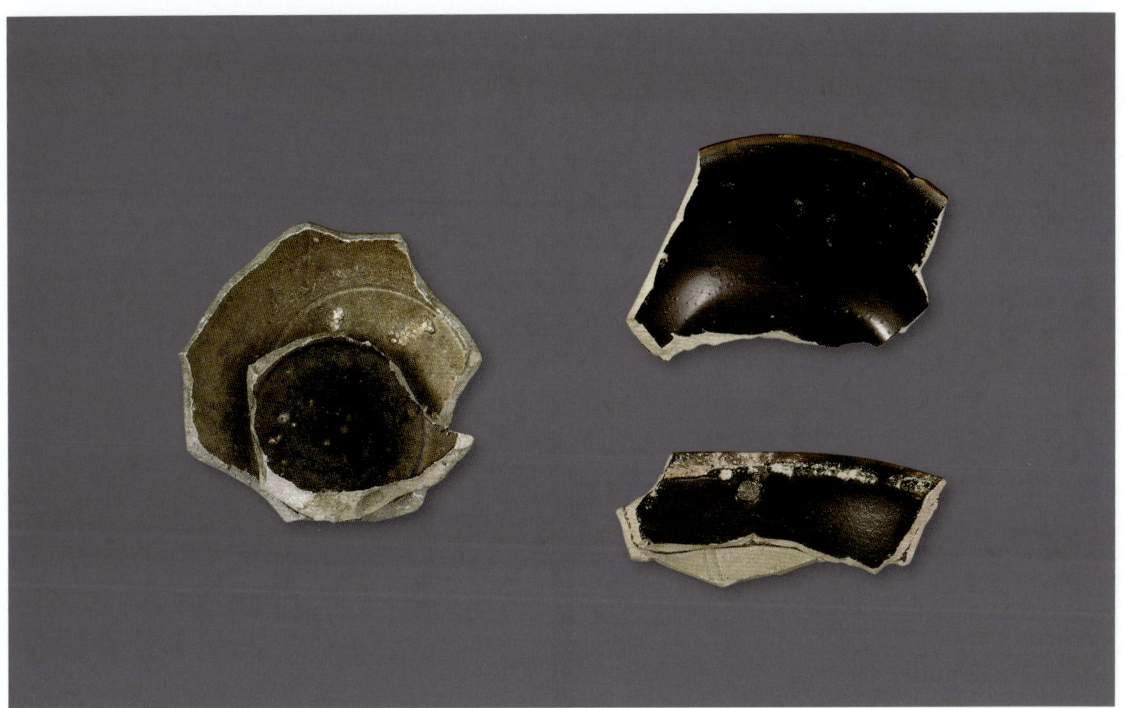

## 877 元 青釉模印菊瓣纹折沿盘标本

Yuan dynasty

Specimens of green glaze plate with everted flange and stamped design of chrysanthemum-petal

878 **宋至元 窑具标本**
From Song dynasty to Yuan dynasty
Specimens of kiln furniture

879 **宋至元 窑具标本**
From Song dynasty to Yuan dynasty
Specimen of kiln furniture

# 兰溪窑

窑址在浙江省兰溪县嵩山，故宫博物院部分专家学者 1981 年、1983 年、2009 年考察了此窑。

水阁公社发现该窑宋代窑址，面积 500 多平方米，堆积层厚 0.8 米。水库边的山坡上堆积有大量匣钵和垫圈，匣钵为 M 形，垫圈大小都有，器物碎片相对较少，其中有不少生烧，胎质疏松，有的手掰即碎。少数遗物具有五代越窑遗风，如浮雕莲瓣碗、圈足外卷小杯与卧足盖盒等；宋代器物胎色浅灰，釉色浅青透明，玻璃质感强，有不少开有细碎片纹，具有独特风格。以壶和碗较多，壶的腹部为扁圆形，多饰六组双凸线，器身造型稳重之中有秀美，壶腹饰细线划花；碗满釉支烧，粗者直接垫烧。还有高式注碗，碗心有放射状花瓣，多刻花装饰，少划花装饰，器外还有多层莲瓣装饰的。莲瓣装饰受越窑影响，遒劲粗放，风格独特。此外还有瓶、罐、卧足钵、盒、盏托、小杯、水盂、莲瓣盘等器物。产品在烧造方法、装饰、造型上与越窑有一定关系。

# Lanxi Kiln

Kiln site is in Songshan, Lanxi County. Experts from the Palace Museum investigated the site in 1981, 1983 and 2009.

A kiln site of Song dynasty was found in Shuige Town. It covers an area of over 500 square meters with accumulation of materials related to the kiln as high as 0.8 meter. A great many saggars and supporting rings were piled up along the slope by the reservoir. Saggars are M – shaped and supporting rings vary in size. Porcelain parts are relatively small in number and many of which were fired unglazed. As a result, the body of the porcelain parts is soft. Some are so soft that they can be crushed into small pieces by hands. A few of the relics have the style of Yue kiln ware of Five Dynasties, for example, bowl with design of lotus-petals in relief, small cup with outward-curving ring foot and box with concave foot. The body of Song dynasty wares is in light gray and the glaze is in light green, transparent and glassy as well. Some are with small crackles in the glaze layer. In a word, wares of Song dynasty are unique. They are mainly pots and bowls. The abdomen of the pot is flat-round-shaped and decorated with six groups of double lines in relief and incised patterns. It looks firm and beautiful. Bowls were completely glazed and fired with spurs. Poor quality bowls were fired using pads. There is another type of bowl which is relatively higher. The inside center of the bowl is decorated with radial petals usually incised and in some cases, carved. The outside was decorated with multi-layer lotus-petals, an influence of Yue kiln. In addition, the kiln fired vases, jars, alms bowls with concave foot, boxes, saucers, small cups, water containers, plates with lotus-petal design, etc. As far as firing techniques, decoration and shaping be concerned, Lanxi kiln was related to Yue kiln.

**兰溪窑遗址**
Ruin of Lanxi kiln

**兰溪窑遗址瓷片遗存**
Pileup of porcelain parts at the ruin of Lanxi kiln

880　五代至宋　青釉壶标本
From Five Dynasties to Song dynasty
Specimens of green glaze pot

881 五代至宋 青釉瓜棱壶标本
From Five Dynasties to Song dynasty
Specimens of green glaze melon-shaped pot

882　**五代至宋　青釉瓜棱壶标本**

From Five Dynasties to Song dynasty

Specimens of green glaze melon-shaped pot

883　五代至宋　青釉瓜棱壶标本
From Five Dynasties to Song dynasty
Specimens of green glaze melon-shaped pot

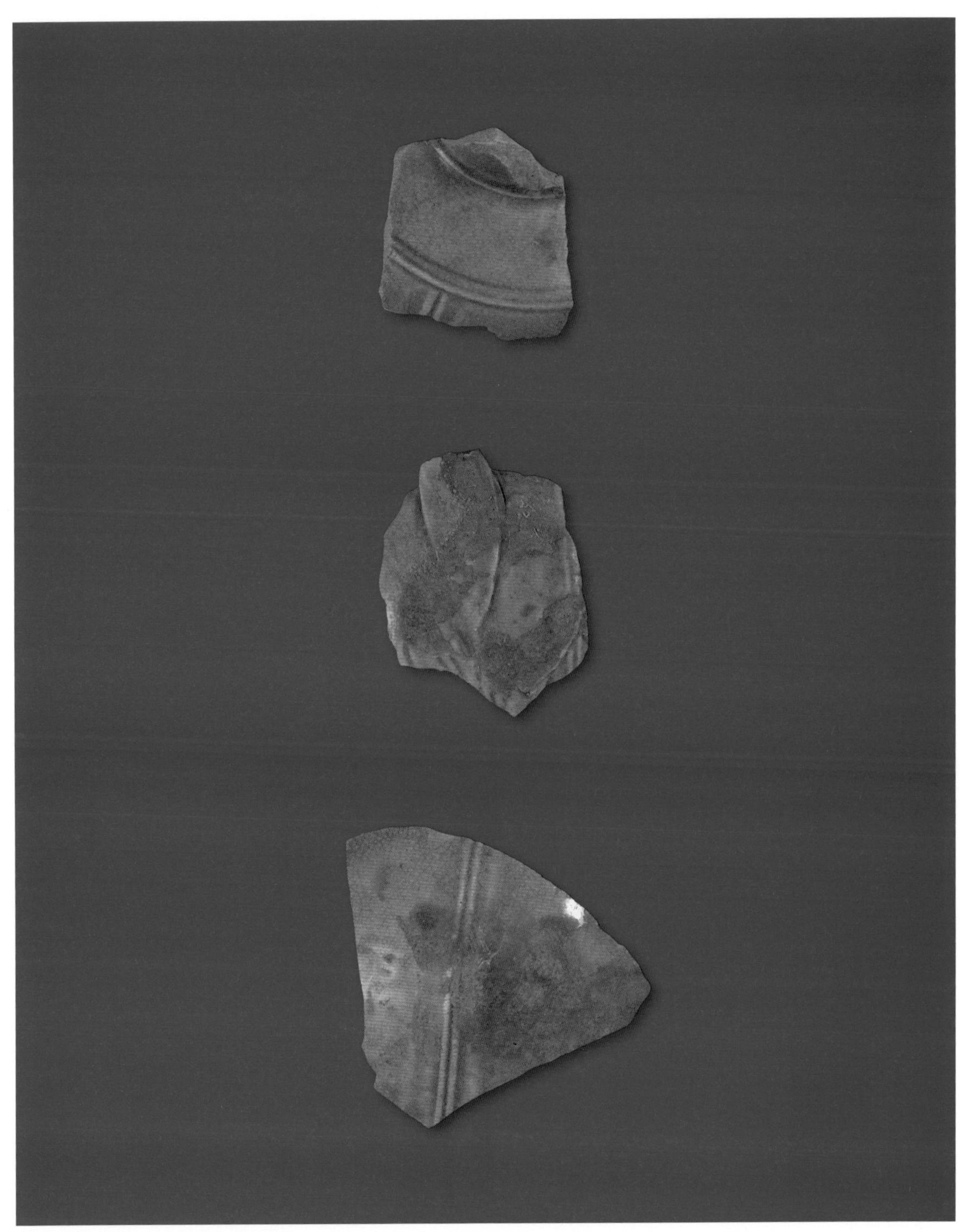

884 **五代至宋 青釉碗标本**

From Five Dynasties to Song dynasty

Specimens of green glaze bowl

## 885 五代至宋 青釉碗标本

From Five Dynasties to Song dynasty

Specimens of green glaze bowl

886 五代至宋 青釉碗标本

From Five Dynasties to Song dynasty

Specimens of green glaze bowl

887　**五代至宋　青釉钵标本**

From Five Dynasties to Song dynasty

Specimens of green glaze alms bowl

888　**五代至宋**

**青釉刻花瓜棱壶标本**

From Five Dynasties to Song dynasty

Specimen of green glaze melon-shaped pot with incised design

889　五代至宋　青釉刻花花瓣纹碗标本
From Five Dynasties to Song dynasty
Specimens of green glaze bowl with incised flower-petal design

890　五代至宋　青釉刻花莲瓣纹碗标本
From Five Dynasties to Song dynasty
Specimens of green glaze bowl with incised lotus-petal design

891　**五代至宋　青釉刻花莲瓣纹碗标本**

From Five Dynasties to Song dynasty

Specimens of green glaze bowl with incised lotus-petal design

892 五代至宋
青釉刻花花瓣纹温碗标本
From Five Dynasties to Song dynasty
Specimen of green glaze warming bowl with incised flower-petal design

893 五代至宋
青釉刻花花瓣纹钵标本
From Five Dynasties to Song dynasty
Specimen of green glaze alms bowl with incised flower-petal design

894 五代至宋 窑具标本
From Five Dynasties to Song dynasty
Specimens of kiln furniture

895 五代至宋 窑具标本
From Five Dynasties to Song dynasty
Specimen of kiln furniture

# 浦江窑

窑址位于浙江省浦江县南约七公里处，已发现宋、元时期窑址。故宫博物院部分专家学者于20世纪80年代、2009年调查了浦江民生、白泥岭窑址。

民生窑。宋代烧青瓷，北宋受越窑影响，釉色青绿，一类胎较白，釉色比越窑鲜艳。有细线划花各式盘、碗、钵，大多釉色精美。器物多采用裹足支烧；另一类胎色灰，釉的呈色比白胎者浓重，制作稍粗。印双荷叶、莲花纹的梅花式小杯与东阳窑产品相似。青釉壶壶身为六等分瓜棱形，线有凹凸两种。元代烧制青釉各式盘、碗，折沿盘大小与龙泉窑盘略同。采用叠烧工艺，质地较粗，圈足较厚。

白泥岭窑。采集的标本有青釉、青黄釉，有的未烧熟。有各式碗、盘、杯、壶等。壶折肩，腹起双凸线。有外刻花者，采集的花瓣纹杯，质量较好，代表了该窑的较高水平。烧造有直接叠烧、垫圈垫烧、匣钵装烧。匣钵种类多，有大小数种，垫圈也是，还有喇叭形垫柱。

# Pujiang Kiln

Pujiang kiln is located about 7 km south of the county town, Pujiang, Zhejiang Province. Kiln sites of Song and Yuan dynasty have been found. Experts from the Palace Museum investigated kiln sites at Minsheng and Bainiling in the 1980s and in 2009.

Green glaze wares were fired in Song dynasty at Minsheng. Influenced by Yue kiln in Northern Song dynasty, the glaze is in bluish green. The glaze color of wares with relatively white body is brighter than that of Yue kiln. Plates, bowls and alms bowls of various kinds are with incised design. Most of them are with delicate glaze. They were fired with supporting tools. The glaze color of poorly made wares with relatively grey body is darker than that of the previous. Plum-shaped small cups with stamped design of two lotus leaves or lotus are similar to that of Dongyang kiln. The body of melon-shaped green glaze pot is consisted of six equal portions. And the joints of the portions are either concave or protruding. Green glaze plates and bowls of various kinds were fired in Yuan dynasty. The size of plates with everted flange is similar to that of Longquan kiln. They were put into kiln one inside the other directly and fired and they are poor in quality and with relatively thick ring foot.

Specimens collected at Bainiling are green glaze and greenish yellow glaze wares, such as bowls, plates, cups, pots, etc. Some of them are immature. Pots are off shoulder and with design of twin lines in relief on belly. Cups with design of flowers collected are of good quality, which could represent the level of the kiln. Wares were put into kiln for firing one inside the other directly or with a supporting ring in between or inside saggars which vary in size and type. So do supporting rings. There are also supporting posts in shape of speakers.

896 **宋 青釉瓜棱壶标本**

Song dynasty

Specimens of green glaze melon-shaped pot

897　宋　青釉瓜棱壶标本
Song dynasty
Specimens of green glaze melon-shaped pot

898　宋　青釉碗标本
Song dynasty
Specimens of green glaze bowl

899　**宋　青釉盏托标本**

Song dynasty

Specimens of green glaze saucer

900　**宋　青釉盘标本**

Song dynasty

Specimen of green glaze plate

901 **宋 青釉花式盘标本**
Song dynasty
Specimen of green glaze flower-shaped plate

902 **宋**
**青釉划花花卉纹壶标本**
Song dynasty
Specimen of green glaze pot with incised floral design

**浦江（白泥岭）窑遗址**
Ruin of Pujiang kiln at Bainiling

**浦江（白泥岭）窑遗址瓷片遗存**
Pileup of porcelain parts at the ruin of Pujiang kiln at Bainiling

903　宋　青釉瓜棱壶标本

Song dynasty

Specimens of green glaze melon-shaped pot

904　**宋　青釉碗标本**

Song dynasty

Specimens of green glaze bowl

905　**宋　青釉碗标本**

Song dynasty

Specimens of green glaze bowl

906　宋　青釉碗标本
Song dynasty
Specimens of green glaze bowl

907　**宋　青釉花式碗标本**

Song dynasty

Specimens of green glaze flower-shaped bowl

908　宋　青釉钵标本
Song dynasty
Specimens of green glaze alms bowl

909　**宋　青釉刻花花瓣纹碗标本**
Song dynasty
Specimen of green glaze bowl
with incised flower-petal design

910　**宋　窑具标本**
Song dynasty
Specimen of kiln furniture

911 宋 窑具标本
Song dynasty
Specimens of kiln furniture

# 金华窑

窑址在浙江省金华县，故宫博物院部分专家学者 20 世纪 80 年代及 2004 年、2008 年调查了部分窑址。

共发现十多处窑址，其中五朱堂窑址遗物中有青釉褐斑器，由此可确定其上限在东晋时期。五朱堂窑址的发现，把这一地区的烧瓷历史提早了四百年左右。

其余各窑以烧青釉为主，三处兼烧黑釉。以碗为主，造型多样，纹饰较简单，多碗里刻划花篦划或篦点纹，外刻直线纹。横塘窑装饰划花篦划纹、复线纹等。元代铁店窑还烧制钧釉器物，有碗、高足碗、盘、鼓钉洗、花盆、罐、瓶等。从窑址标本看，金华窑器物主要采用垫饼、支圈、支珠垫烧。有些器物碗心留有支烧痕迹。

# Jinhua Kiln

Jinhua kiln is located in Jinhua County, Zhejiang Province. A dozen of kiln sites have been found so far. Experts from the Palace Museum investigated some of the kiln sites in the 1980s, in 2004 and 2008.

The unearthed green glaze with brown spots from Wuzhutang kiln site suggests that the upper limit of the kiln is Eastern Jin dynasty. The discovery of Wuzhutang kiln site makes the firing history of Wuzhou kiln about four hundred years longer.

The rest of kilns fired green glaze wares mainly. Three of the kilns fired black glaze as well. Produce of the kilns are predominantly bowls of various kinds with relatively simple decoration, usually with incised design or comb-incised patterns inside and incised lines outside. Wares of Hengtang kiln are decorated with incised patterns, comb-incised patterns and lines. Tiedian kiln of Yuan dynasty also fired Jun glaze wares, such as bowls, plates, bowls with high stems, washers with drum nail design, flower pots, vases, etc. Specimens indicate Jinhua kiln used mainly pads, support rings and balls to fire wares separately. Marks left behind in the centers of some of the wares, for instance, bowls are the results of the firing technique.

**金华（横塘）窑遗址**
Ruin of Jinhua kiln at Hengtang

912　**宋　青釉碗标本**

Song dynasty

Specimens of green glaze bowl

913　**宋　青釉刻线纹碗标本**

Song dynasty

Specimens of green glaze bowl with incised line design

914　宋　青釉里刻划花篦点纹外刻线纹碗标本

Song dynasty

Specimen of green glaze bowl with design of comb-incised dots inside and incised lines outside

915 宋 青釉划花篦划纹碗标本

Song dynasty

Specimens of green glaze bowl with design of comb-incised patterns

## 916 宋 青釉划花篦划纹碗标本

Song dynasty

Specimens of green glaze bowl with design of comb-incised patterns

917　**宋　青釉划花篦划纹盘标本**
Song dynasty
Specimen of green glaze plate with design of comb-incised patterns

918　**宋　窑具标本**
Song dynasty
Specimen of kiln furniture

**金华（铁店）窑遗址瓷片遗存**

Pileup of porcelain parts at the ruin of Jinhua kiln at Tiedian

919 宋

**青釉印“天下太平”铭碗标本**

Song dynasty

Specimen of green glaze bowl with stamped Chinese characters Tian Xia Tai Ping

920 宋

**青釉刻划花篦划纹碗标本**

Song dynasty

Specimen of green glaze bowl with comb-incised design

## 921 宋 青釉里刻划花篦划纹外刻线纹碗标本

Song dynasty

Specimens of green glaze bowl with comb-incised design inside and incised lines outside

922 宋 青釉里刻划花篦划纹外刻线纹碗标本

Song dynasty

Specimens of green glaze bowl with comb-incised design inside and incised lines outside

923 宋 青釉里刻划花篦划纹外刻线纹碗标本

Song dynasty

Specimen of green glaze bowl with comb-incised design inside and incised lines outside

924　宋　青釉里划花篦划纹外刻线纹碗标本
Song dynasty
Specimen of green glaze bowl with comb-incised design inside and incised lines outside

925　宋　黑釉罐标本
Song dynasty
Specimen of black glaze jar

926 **宋　酱釉罐标本**
Song dynasty
Specimen of dark brown glaze jar

927 **宋　酱釉壶标本**
Song dynasty
Specimen of dark brown glaze pot

928 **宋　酱釉鼓钉纹罐标本**
Song dynasty
Specimen of dark brown glaze jar with drum-nail design

929　元　钧釉瓶标本
Yuan dynasty
Specimen of Jun glaze vase

930　元　钧釉瓶标本
Yuan dynasty
Specimen of Jun glaze vase

931　元　钧釉罐标本
Yuan dynasty
Specimen of Jun glaze jar

932　元　钧釉炉标本
Yuan dynasty
Specimen of Jun glaze burner

933　元　钧釉三足炉标本
Yuan dynasty
Specimens of Jun glaze burner with three-legged design

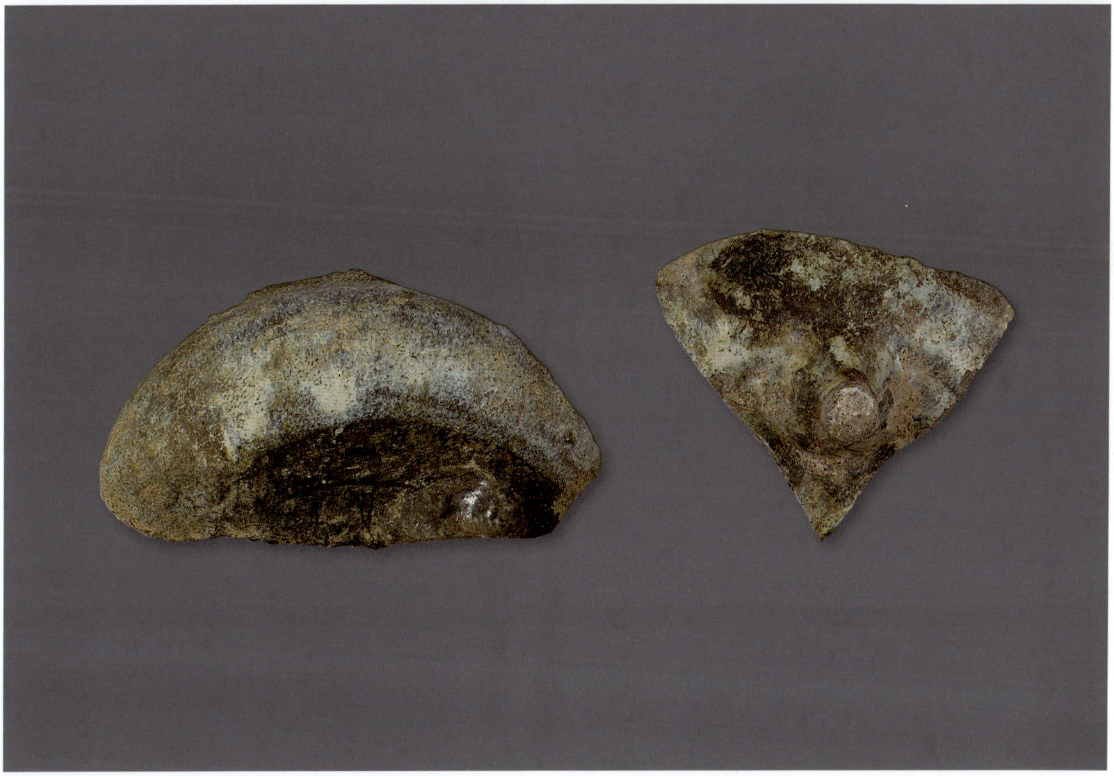

934　元　钧釉碗标本

Yuan dynasty

Specimens of Jun glaze bowl

935 **元 钧釉碗标本**

Yuan dynasty

Specimens of Jun glaze bowl

936　元　钧釉碗标本
Yuan dynasty
Specimens of Jun glaze bowl

937　元　钧釉碗标本
Yuan dynasty
Specimen of Jun glaze bowl

938 元 钧釉碗标本
Yuan dynasty
Specimens of Jun glaze bowl

939　元　钧釉碗标本

Yuan dynasty

Specimens of Jun glaze bowl

940　元　钧釉高足杯标本

Yuan dynasty

Specimens of Jun glaze cup with high stem

## 941　元　钧釉弦纹花盆标本

Yuan dynasty

Specimen of Jun glaze flower pot with strings

附图

**元　钧釉弦纹花口花盆**

高 19.8 厘米

Illustration

Yuan dynasty

Jun glaze flower pot with flower rim and strings

Height 19.8cm

花盆花口外折，口以下渐内收，腹部饰两道凸弦纹，下腹部饰有花边装饰，至近足出凸棱一道。器外施窑变花釉不到底，釉色蓝白深浅相间，色较河南钧釉为暗。器里施釉至口以下，下部露胎。

此类花盆见于韩国新安海底沉船，说明该窑产品元代外销。

942 元 钧釉弦纹花口花盆标本

Yuan dynasty

Specimens of Jun glaze flower pot with flower rim and strings

943　元　钧釉鼓钉纹三足洗标本

Yuan dynasty

Specimens of Jun glaze washer with drum-nail and three-legged design

944　元　钧釉刻划花碗标本

Yuan dynasty

Specimens of Jun glaze bowl with incised design

# 武义窑

窑址在浙江省武义县境内，未见文献记载。目前已发现几十处窑址，故宫博物院部分专家学者20世纪70年代、2004年、2008年调查了门牛山、小窑、新窑、蜈蚣山、瓦灶山、黄茅山、郭洞等处窑址。

武义窑绝大部分为宋代遗址，以烧青瓷为主，碗里多刻划花兼篦点纹饰，碗心有刻团菊纹者，碗外刻线纹，与龙泉窑同类装饰相似，质量较好。

郭洞窑遗存较为丰富，采集有宋代青釉、黑釉，元代青釉标本。元代瓷窑多烧制龙泉风格青釉盘、碗，碗心以印阴文花卉居多，有于花卉空隙印八思巴文者，但发现数量不多。此外，在窑址中还采集到钧釉碗、盘标本，与金华铁店窑同类器物相似。

# Wuyi Kiln

Wuyi kiln is located in Wuyi County, Zhejiang Province. It is not documented literarily. Dozens of kiln sites have been found across the county so far. Experts from the Palace Museum investigated kiln sites at Menniushan, Xiaoyao, Wugongshan, Wazaoshan, Huangmaoshan, Guodong, etc. in the 1970s, in 2004 and 2008.

Wuyi kiln sites are mostly of Song dynasty. Produce of the kiln are mainly green glaze. Bowls with incised design of comb dots inside, medallion of chrysanthemum in the center and double lines outside are similar to that of Longquan kiln in term of decoration and they are of better quality. Relics at Guodong site are abundant. Specimens collected include green and black glaze of Song dynasty and green glaze of Yuan dynasty. Kilns of Yuan dynasty fired mostly green glaze plates and bowls of Longquan kiln style. The center of bowls is usually with stamped design of flora in negative legend. Some of the bowls are with stamped design of Phags-ba script in between flora in inside center. In addition, specimens of Jun glaze bowl and plate were also collected at the kiln site, which are similar to that of Jinhua kiln at Tiedian.

945 宋 青釉碗标本

Song dynasty

Specimen of green glaze bowl

946 宋 青釉印花花卉纹碗标本

Song dynasty

Specimen of green glaze bowl with stamped floral design

947 **宋　青釉折沿盘标本**
Song dynasty
Specimen of green glaze plate with everted flange

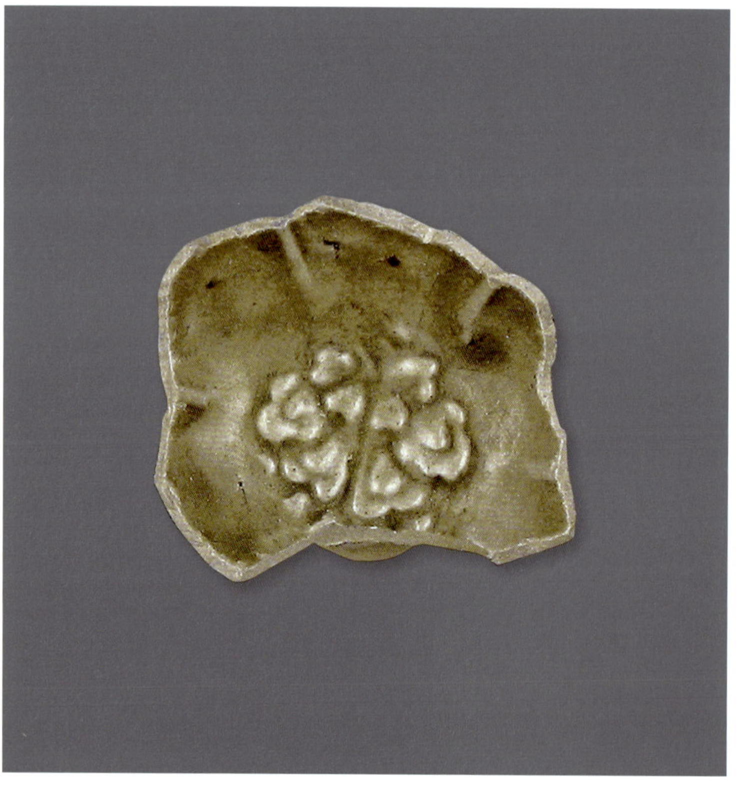

948 **宋**
**青釉印花花卉纹花式碗标本**
Song dynasty
Specimen of green glaze flower-shaped bowl with stamped flower design

949 宋 青釉刻花莲瓣纹瓶标本
Song dynasty
Specimen of green glaze vase with incised lotus-petal design

950 宋 青釉刻花瓜棱壶标本
Song dynasty
Specimen of green glaze melon-shaped pot with incised design

951 宋 青釉刻花花卉纹碗标本
Song dynasty
Specimen of green glaze bowl with incised flower design

952　宋

**青釉划花篦划纹碗标本**

Song dynasty

Specimen of green glaze bowl with comb-incised design

953　宋

**青釉划花篦划纹碗标本**

Song dynasty

Specimen of green glaze bowl with comb-incised design

954　**宋**

**青釉划花篦划纹碗标本**

Song dynasty

Specimen of green glaze bowl with comb-incised design

955　**宋**

**青釉划花篦划团花纹碗标本**

Song dynasty

Specimen of green glaze bowl with incised medallion design

956 宋 青釉里刻划花篦点团菊纹外刻线纹碗标本

Song dynasty

Specimens of green glaze bowl with comb-incised design of dots and medallion of chrysanthemum inside and incised lines outside

957　宋　青釉里划花篦划纹外刻线纹碗标本

Song dynasty

Specimens of green glaze bowl with comb-incised design inside and incised line design outside

958 宋 青釉里划花篦点纹外刻线纹碗标本

Song dynasty

Specimens of green glaze bowl with comb-incised dot design inside and incised line design outside

959 宋 青釉划花花卉纹盘标本
Song dynasty
Specimen of green glaze plate with
incised floral design

960 宋 青釉划花篦划纹盘标本
Song dynasty
Specimen of green glaze plate with
comb-incised design

961 宋 青釉划花篦划纹盘标本
Song dynasty
Specimen of green glaze plate with
comb-incised design

962　宋　青釉划花篦点纹盘标本

Song dynasty

Specimen of green glaze plate with comb-incised dot design

963　宋　窑具标本

Song dynasty

Specimen of kiln furniture

964 **宋 青釉壶标本**
Song dynasty
Specimen of green glaze pot

965 **宋 青釉瓜棱壶标本**
Song dynasty
Specimen of green glaze melon-shaped pot

966　宋　青釉盒标本
Song dynasty
Specimen of green glaze box

967　宋　青釉器盖标本
Song dynasty
Specimen of green glaze cover

968　宋　青釉里刻划花篦划纹外刻线纹碗标本

Song dynasty

Specimens of green glaze bowl with comb-incised design inside and incised line design outside

969　**宋　黑釉碗标本**
Song dynasty
Specimens of black glaze bowl

970　**宋　青釉碗标本**

Song dynasty

Specimens of green glaze bowl

971 宋 青釉刻线纹碗标本
Song dynasty
Specimen of green glaze bowl with incised line design

972 宋 青釉刻划花碗标本
Song dynasty
Specimen of green glaze bowl with incised design

973　**宋　黑釉碗标本**

Song dynasty

Specimens of black glaze bowl

974　南宋至元　钧釉碗标本
From Southern Song to Yuan dynasty
Specimens of Jun glaze bowl

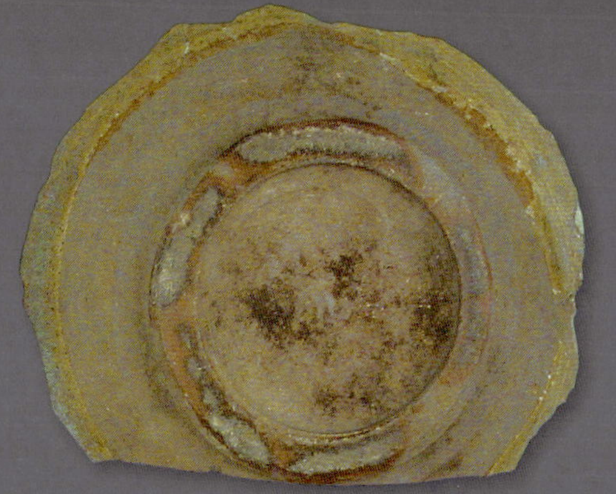

975　元　青釉碗标本

Yuan dynasty

Specimens of green glaze bowl

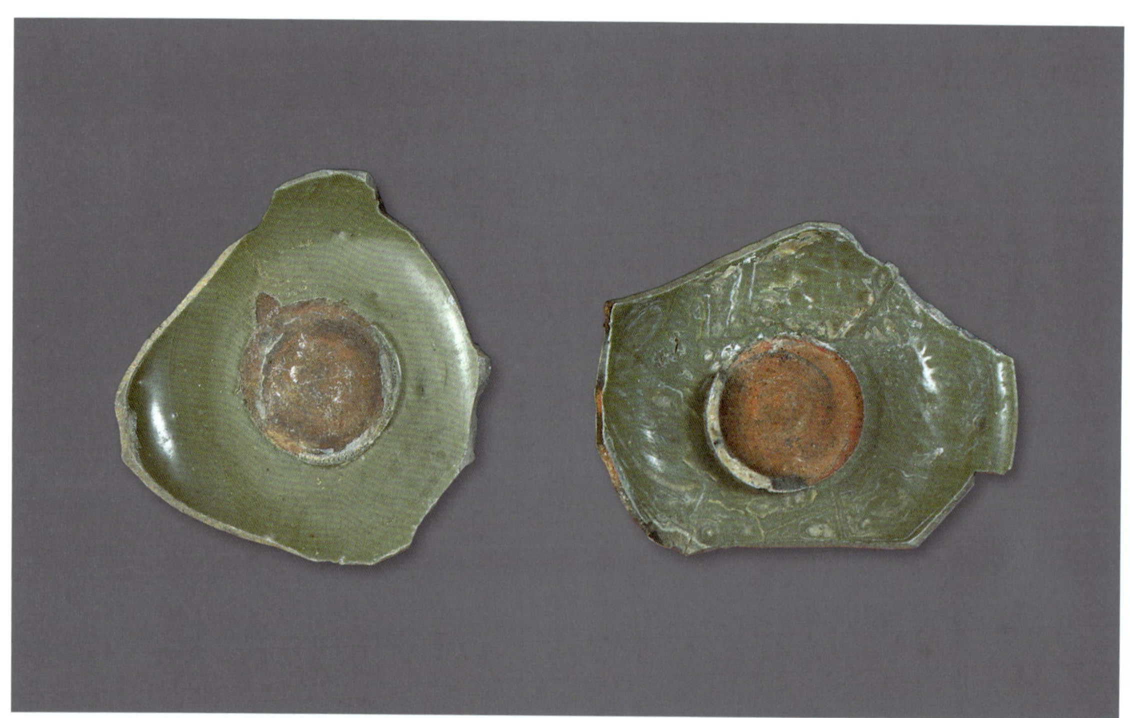

976 元 青釉碗标本
Yuan dynasty
Specimen of green glaze bowl

977 元 青釉碗标本
Yuan dynasty
Specimen of green glaze bowl

978　元　青釉盘标本

Yuan dynasty

Specimens of green glaze plate

979　宋　青釉里刻划花篦划纹外刻线纹碗标本

Song dynasty

Specimens of green glaze bowl with comb-incised design inside and incised line design outside

980　元　青釉碗标本

Yuan dynasty

Specimens of green glaze bowl

981　元　青釉盘标本

Yuan dynasty

Specimen of green glaze plate

**武义（郭洞）窑遗址**

Ruin of Wuyi kiln at Guodong

982　元　青釉碗标本
Yuan dynasty
Specimens of green glaze bowl

983　元　青釉碗标本

Yuan dynasty

Specimens of green glaze bowl

984　元　**青釉碗标本**
Yuan dynasty
Specimen of green glaze bowl

985　元　**青釉盘标本**
Yuan dynasty
Specimen of green glaze plate

## 986　元　青釉印花花卉纹碗标本

Yuan dynasty

Specimens of green glaze bowl with stamped flower design

987　元　青釉印花花卉纹盘标本

Yuan dynasty

Specimens of green glaze plate with stamped flower design

## 988 元 青釉印花花卉纹盘标本

Yuan dynasty

Specimens of green glaze plate with stamped flower design

989　元　窑具标本

Yuan dynasty

Specimens of kiln furniture

990 **宋 青釉盘标本**
Song dynasty
Specimen of green glaze plate

991 **宋 青釉折沿盘标本**
Song dynasty
Specimens of green glaze plate with everted flange

992　宋　青釉里刻花篦划团菊纹外刻线纹碗标本

Song dynasty　Specimens of green glaze bowl with comb-incised design of medallion of chrysanthemum inside and incised lines outside

993　宋　青釉里刻花篦点团菊纹外刻线纹碗标本

Song dynasty　Specimens of green glaze bowl with comb-incised design of dots and medallion of chrysanthemum inside and incised lines outside

994　**宋　青釉里刻划花篦划纹外刻线纹碗标本**

Song dynasty

Specimens of green glaze bowl with comb-incised design inside and incised lines outside

995　宋　青釉里刻划花篦划纹外刻线纹碗标本
Song dynasty
Specimen of green glaze bowl with comb-incised design inside and incised lines outside

996　宋　青釉刻划花花卉纹盘标本
Song dynasty
Specimen of green glaze plate with incised floral design

997　宋　青釉刻划花花卉纹盘标本

Song dynasty

Specimens of green glaze plate with incised floral design

998　**宋　青釉刻划花花卉纹盘标本**

Song dynasty

Specimen of green glaze plate with incised floral design

999　宋　青釉里划花篦点纹外刻线纹碗标本

Song dynasty

Specimens of green glaze bowl with comb-incised dot design inside and incised lines outside

1000 **宋　青釉划花篦划花瓣纹盘标本**

Song dynasty

Specimen of green glaze plate with comb-incised flower-petal design

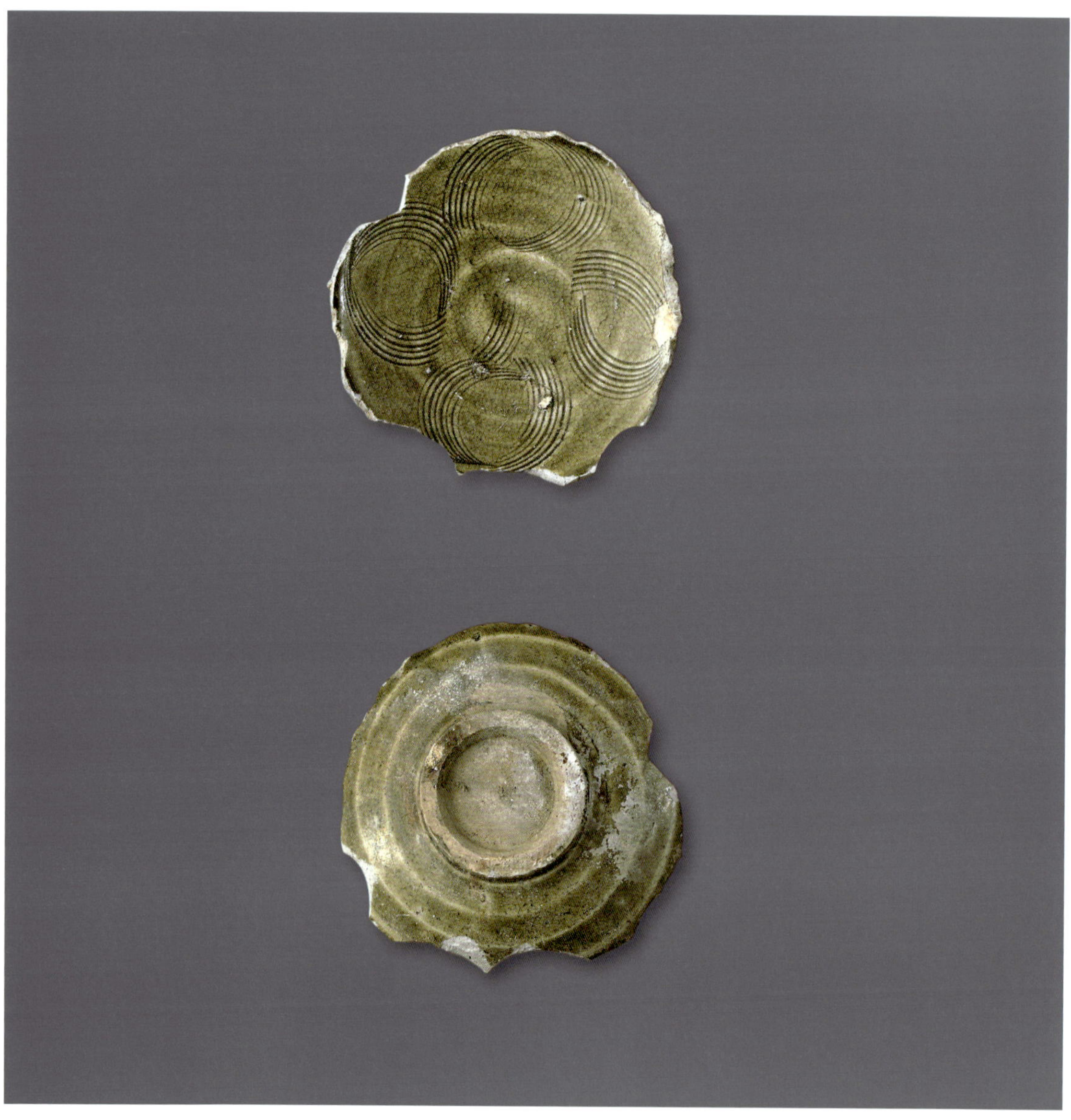

1001 **宋 青釉划花篦划花瓣纹折沿盘标本**

Song dynasty

Specimens of green glaze plate with comb-incised flower-petal design and everted flange

1002 **宋 黑釉碗标本**

Song dynasty

Specimens of black glaze bowl

1003 **宋 黑釉碗标本**

Song dynasty

Specimens of black glaze bowl

1004 **宋　窑具标本**
Song dynasty
Specimens of kiln furniture

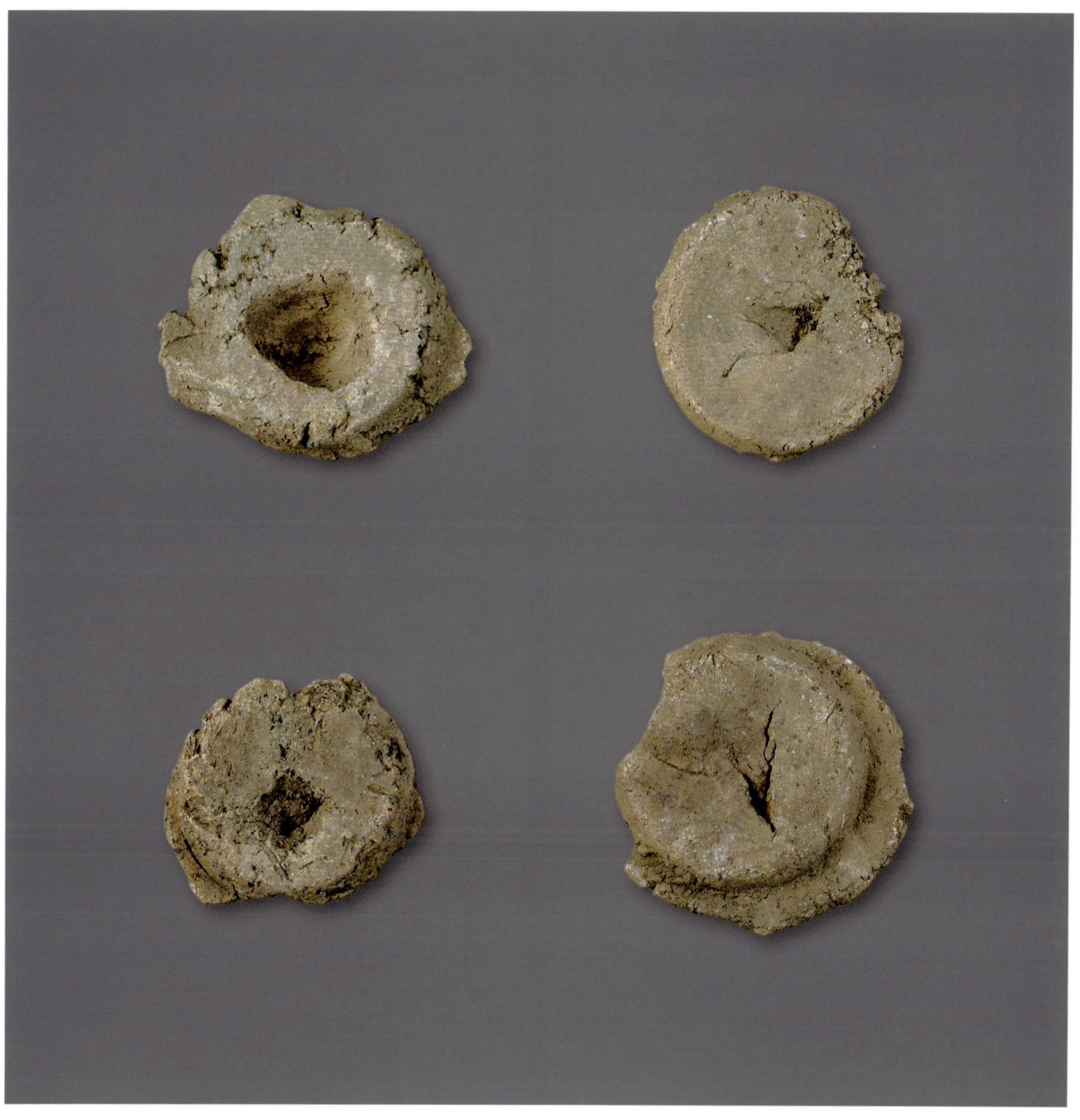

1005 **宋 黑釉碗标本**

Song dynasty

Specimens of black glaze bowl

1006 **宋 黑釉碗标本**

Song dynasty

Specimens of black glaze bowl

1007 **宋 黑釉碗标本**

Song dynasty

Specimens of black glaze bowl

# 义乌窑

2009 年 12 月，故宫博物院部分专家学者调查了义乌的葛塘碗窑山窑址与竹山里窑址群。

葛塘碗窑山窑。以烧造青釉为主，釉色有青绿、青黄。装饰有划花、划花篦划纹。碗心多有垫烧痕。有的直接垫烧，看不到支具。发现有匣钵，但质地疏松，多成碎块，垫柱也有少量发现。垫饼多不规则，随意捏就。有些器物造型、胎釉、装饰似金华窑、武义窑青釉器物。

竹山里窑址群。在义乌市东碗窑村（李唐村）。烧造钧釉为主，兼少量青、褐釉。器类以碗为主，有少量钵、折沿盘。窑具很少，似直接叠烧，碗心留有叠烧痕，与金华铁店窑、武义窑产品相似。

# Yiwu Kiln

Experts from the Palace Museum investigated Yiwu kiln sites at Zhushanli and Wanyaoshan, Getang in December, 2009.

Kiln at Wanyaoshan, Getang fired mainly green glaze wares with incised design of flora or comb patterns. Glaze is in bluish green and greenish yellow. Inside the center of bowls, marks of direct contacts of bowls when fired were left behind. No supporting tools were found. The saggars found are in small parts and their texture is loose. There are a few column-shaped pads found. The shape of pads is irregular. They might be made listening to hearts. As far as shaping, body and glaze, decoration be concerned, some of the wares are similar to those of Jinhua and Wuyi kiln.

Zhushanli is located at Dongwanyao (Litang) Village, Yiwu City. It refers to a group of kiln sites. The kiln mainly fired Jun glaze wares. It also fired a small number of green glaze and brown glaze wares. Its main produce is bowls. Apart from bowls, it fired a small number of alms bowls and plates with everted flange. There is few kiln furniture found, which might suggest the wares were put into the kiln one inside the other directly and fired. As a result, marks of direct contacts of wares were left by at the center of bowls. Its firing technique is similar to that of Jinhua kiln at Tiedian and Wuyi kiln.

**义乌（葛塘碗窑山）窑遗址保护牌**

Monument for protecting the ruin of Yiwu kiln at Wanyaoshan, Getang

1008　**宋　青釉碗标本**

Song dynasty

Specimens of green glaze bowl

1009 **宋 青釉刻划花纹碗标本**

Song dynasty

Specimens of green glaze bowl with incised design

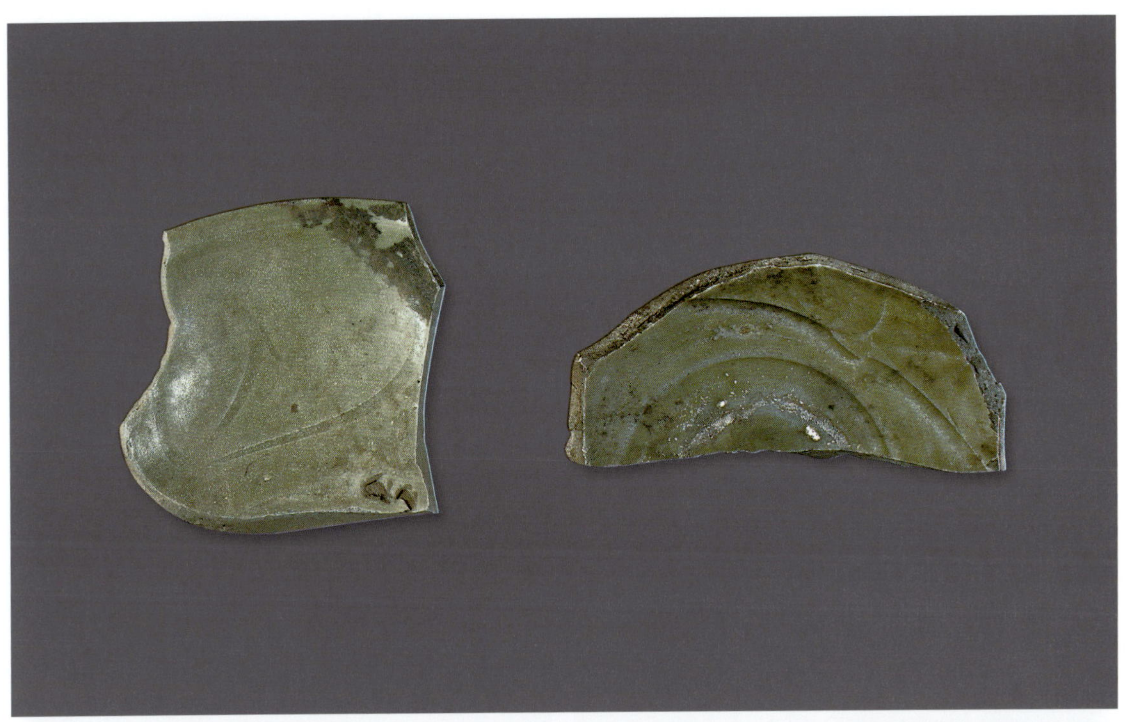

1010 **宋　青釉刻划花纹碗标本**

Song dynasty

Specimens of green glaze bowl with incised design

1011　宋　青釉里刻划花外刻线纹碗标本

Song dynasty

Specimen of green glaze bowl with incised design inside and incised lines outside

1012 **宋　青釉里刻划花外刻线纹碗标本**

Song dynasty

Specimens of green glaze bowl with incised design inside and incised lines outside

## 1013　宋　青釉里刻划花外刻线纹碗标本

Song dynasty

Specimens of green glaze bowl with incised design inside and incised lines outside

1014 宋 青釉里刻划花外刻线纹碗标本
Song dynasty Specimen of green glaze bowl with incised design inside and incised lines outside

1015 宋 青釉里刻划花外篦划纹碗标本
Song dynasty Specimen of green glaze bowl with incised design inside and comb-incised design outside

1016 **宋至元　青釉盘标本**

From Song dynasty to Yuan dynasty

Specimens of green glaze plate

1017 **宋至元 窑具标本**

From Song dynasty to Yuan dynasty

Specimen of kiln furniture

**义乌（竹山里）窑遗址**

Ruin of Yiwu kiln at Zhushanli

1018 **南宋至元 钧釉碗标本**

From Southern Song dynasty to Yuan dynasty

Specimens of Jun glaze bowl

1019 **南宋至元　钧釉碗标本**

From Southern Song dynasty to Yuan dynasty

Specimens of Jun glaze bowl

1020　**南宋至元　钧釉碗标本**

From Southern Song dynasty to Yuan dynasty

Specimens of Jun glaze bowl

1021 **南宋至元 钧釉碗标本**

From Southern Song dynasty to Yuan dynasty

Specimens of Jun glaze bowl

1022　**南宋至元　钧釉碗标本**

From Southern Song dynasty to Yuan dynasty

Specimens of Jun glaze bowl

1023　南宋至元　钧釉碗标本
From Southern Song dynasty to Yuan dynasty
Specimens of Jun glaze bowl

1024 **南宋至元　钧釉碗标本**

From Southern Song dynasty to Yuan dynasty

Specimens of Jun glaze bowl

1025 **南宋至元　钧釉刻线纹碗标本**
From Southern Song dynasty to Yuan dynasty
Specimens of Jun glaze bowl with incised line design

1026 **南宋至元　青褐釉碗标本**

From Southern Song dynasty to Yuan dynasty

Specimens of bluish brown glaze bowl

1027 **南宋至元 褐釉碗标本**

From Southern Song dynasty to Yuan dynasty

Specimens of brown glaze bowl

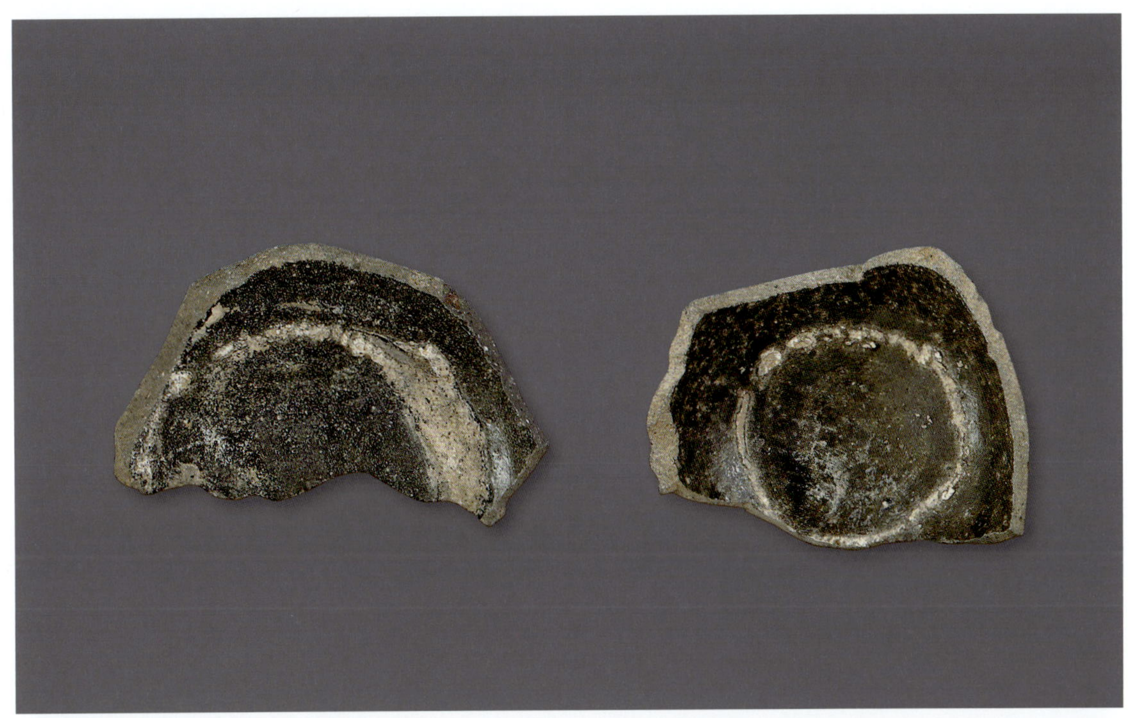

# 永康窑

窑址在永康县境内，属宋代瓷窑。故宫博物院部分专家学者20世纪80年代、2008年调查了赵店碗金堆、瑶坛窑址。

窑址遗物以碗、盘为主，还有杯、壶、盒、炉等。装饰多样，有印花盒、篦划纹碗、刻花杯、刻线纹炉。篦划纹碗中有外刻线纹的珠光青瓷。有些碗直接叠烧，碗心留有叠烧的圆形支烧痕。此窑的釉色、装饰花纹以及工艺特征与金华窑极为相似；六等分线纹壶与慈溪等窑器物风格相同；五出口杯较高，也是浙江地区常见的造型，其中釉色好者与越窑器物很相近。

# Yongkang Kiln

Yongkang kiln is located in Yongkang County, Zhejiang Province. It is a porcelain kiln of Song dynasty. Experts from the Palace Museum investigated kiln sites at Wanjindui and Yaotan of Zhaodian in the 1980s and in 2008.

Relics found at the kiln sites are mainly bowls, plates and cups, as well as pots, boxes, burners, etc. Decoration methods and products of the kiln are diverse, for instance, box with stamped design, bowl with design of comb-incised patterns, cup with incised design, burner with incised line design. Of the bowls with comb-incised patterns, there is one kind of green glaze with luster of pearl and double lines incised outside. Some bowls were put into the kiln and fired one directly inside the other, thus in the centers round spur marks were left behind. Glaze, decorative patterns and firing techniques of the kiln are very much similar to that of Jinhua kiln. The style of pot with dividing lines of six equal portions is just the same as that of Cixi kiln. Cups in the shape of five flower petals, a common type of ware in Zhejiang Province, are relatively higher. The glaze of the better ones is similar to that of Yue kiln.

**永康（赵店碗金堆）窑遗址**
Ruin of Yongkang kiln
at Zhaodianwanjindui

**永康（赵店碗金堆）窑遗址瓷片遗存**
Pileup of porcelain parts at the ruin of Yongkang kiln at Zhaodianwanjindui

1028　**宋　青釉壶标本**

Song dynasty

Specimens of green glaze pot

1029　**宋　青釉瓜棱壶标本**

Song dynasty

Specimen of green glaze melon-shaped pot

1030 **宋　青釉瓜棱壶标本**
Song dynasty
Specimens of green glaze melon-shaped pot

1031 **宋　青釉瓜棱壶标本**
Song dynasty
Specimens of green glaze melon-shaped pot

1032 **宋　青釉碗标本**

Song dynasty

Specimens of green glaze bowl

1033　**宋　青釉浅碗标本**

Song dynasty

Specimens of green glaze shallow bowl

1034　**宋　青釉花式碗标本**

Song dynasty

Specimens of green glaze flower-shaped bowl

1035　**宋　青釉花式碗标本**
Song dynasty
Specimen of green glaze flower-shaped bowl

1036　**宋　青釉刻花罐标本**
Song dynasty
Specimen of green glaze jar with incised design

1037　宋　青釉刻花罐标本

Song dynasty

Specimen of green glaze jar with incised design

1038　宋　青釉刻花花瓣纹碗标本

Song dynasty

Specimen of green glaze bowl with incised flower-petal design

1039 **宋　青釉刻花放射纹碗标本**

Song dynasty

Specimens of green glaze bowl with incised design of rays

1040 **宋 窑具标本**

Song dynasty

Specimens of kiln furniture

1041 **宋 窑具标本**
Song dynasty
Specimens of kiln furniture

1042 **宋 窑具标本**
Song dynasty
Specimen of kiln furniture

1043　宋　青釉带系罐标本

Song dynasty

Specimen of green glaze jar with handles

1044　**宋　青釉碗标本**

Song dynasty

Specimens of green glaze bowl

1045 **宋　青釉碗标本**

Song dynasty

Specimens of green glaze bowl

1046 **宋 青釉盘标本**
Song dynasty
Specimen of green glaze plate

1047 **宋 青釉刻花五瓣花纹碗标本**
Song dynasty Specimen of green glaze bowl with incised design of five-petaled flower

1048 **宋　青釉刻花莲瓣纹碗标本**

Song dynasty

Specimens of green glaze bowl with incised lotus-petal design

1049 **宋 青釉刻花莲瓣纹碗标本**
Song dynasty
Specimen of green glaze bowl with incised lotus-petal design

1050 **宋 青釉刻线纹碗标本**
Song dynasty
Specimen of green glaze bowl with incised line design

1051　宋　青釉刻花篦划五瓣花纹碗标本

Song dynasty　Specimen of green glaze bowl with comb-incised design of five-petaled flower

1052　宋　青釉刻划花纹碗标本

Song dynasty

Specimen of green glaze bowl with incised design

1053 **宋　青釉刻划花篦划纹碗标本**

Song dynasty

Specimens of green glaze bowl with comb-incised design

1054 **宋　青釉刻划花篦划纹碗标本**

Song dynasty

Specimens of green glaze bowl with comb-incised design

1055　宋　青釉刻划花篦划纹碗标本

Song dynasty

Specimens of green glaze bowl with comb-incised design

1056　**宋　青釉划花篦划纹碗标本**

Song dynasty

Specimens of green glaze bowl with comb-incised design

1057　**宋　青釉里划花篦划纹外刻线纹碗标本**

Song dynasty

Specimen of green glaze bowl with comb-incised design inside and incised line design outside

1058 **宋　青釉划花篦划纹盘标本**
Song dynasty
Specimen of green glaze plate with comb-incised design

1059 **宋　窑具标本**
Song dynasty
Specimen of kiln furniture

1060 **宋　青釉壶标本**
Song dynasty
Specimen of green glaze pot

1061 **宋　青釉瓜棱壶标本**
Song dynasty
Specimen of green glaze melon-shaped pot

1062 **宋 青釉碗标本**

Song dynasty

Specimens of green glaze bowl

1063　宋
**青釉刻花花瓣纹壶标本**
Song dynasty
Specimen of green glaze pot with incised flower-petal design

1064　宋
**青釉刻花莲瓣纹壶标本**
Song dynasty
Specimen of green glaze pot with incised lotus-petal design

1065 **宋 青釉刻线纹碗标本**

Song dynasty

Specimens of green glaze bowl with incised line design

1066 宋 青釉刻线纹杯标本

Song dynasty

Specimen of green glaze cup with incised line design

1067 **宋　青釉刻划花篦划纹碗标本**

Song dynasty

Specimens of green glaze bowl with comb-incised design

1068 **宋 青釉刻划花篦划纹碗标本**

Song dynasty

Specimens of green glaze bowl with comb-incised design

1069 **宋　青釉刻划花篦划纹碗标本**

Song dynasty

Specimens of green glaze bowl with comb-incised design

1070　**宋　青釉刻划花篦划纹碗标本**

Song dynasty

Specimens of green glaze bowl with comb-incised design

1071 **宋　青釉划花篦划纹碗标本**
Song dynasty
Specimens of green glaze bowl with comb-incised design

1072 **宋　青釉划花篦划纹碗标本**
Song dynasty
Specimens of green glaze bowl with comb-incised design

1073 **宋 青釉里划花篦划纹外刻线碗标本**

Song dynasty

Specimen of green glaze bowl with comb-incised design inside and incised line design outside